AF226144

WITNESS

An Oral History of Black Politics in Boston 1920-1960

By Lance Carden

WIPF *&* STOCK · Eugene, Oregon

Resource Publications
A division of Wipf and Stock Publishers
199 W 8th Ave, Suite 3
Eugene, OR 97401

Witness
An Oral History of Black Politics in Boston 1920-1960
By Carden, Lance
Copyright © 1989 by Carden, Lance All rights reserved.
Softcover ISBN-13: 978-1-6667-5996-9
Hardcover ISBN-13: 978-1-6667-5997-6
eBook ISBN-13: 978-1-6667-5998-3
Publication date 10/20/2022
Previously published by Boston College, 1989

This edition is a scanned facsimile of the original edition published in 1989.

This book was commissioned by the African-American Studies Department, Boston College, Amanda Houston, Director. It was funded in part by the Massachusetts Foundation for Humanities and Public Policy and the Massachusetts Council on the Arts and Humanities as part of the fifth Blacks in Boston Conference, April 17 and 18, 1989, sponsored by Boston College, the Museum of Afro-American History, and Roxbury Community College.

Acknowledgments

I want to thank everyone who participated in the interviews. I hope this manuscript repays, at least in part, your investment of time and energy. I also wish to acknowledge the generous support and contributions from Boston College, in particular Rev. William B. Neenan, SJ; Robert Barth, SJ; and Dr. Francis B. Campanella, Executive Director.

I am also indebted to Robert C. Hayden, who provided valuable historical information and technical assistance in oral history interviewing, to Ben Birnbaum of Boston College Magazine, who helped give shape to the narrative, John J. McElligott, Executive Secretary of the Boston Board of Election Commissioners, who helped me verify election data; to Jonathan Cooper-Wiele and Richard Harley, two important role models; to David and Merelice England, who offered early encouragement; to Gary Zabel and Diane Dana, who read and critiqued early versions of the manuscript; to John and Elsa Bengel, who provided some needed space and equipment; to Sandra Sandeford and the staff of the Black Studies Department at Boston College for much appreciated clerical support — and, most of all, to Amanda Houston, who somehow knew intuitively that I would respond positively to a great opportunity. Thank you, all.

Lance Carden
March 1989

Table of Contents

Cover photos by Gordon Gaul include (clockwise from upper left): Edward L. Cooper, the Rev. Michael Haynes, Elma Lewis, Amanda Houston.

Author's Note

This historical narrative has a two-fold significance:

First, it is the first published history covering the Black experience in Boston from the First World War to the tumultuous 1960s. Some of the events of the '50s — particularly urban renewal in the South End — are discussed in Mel King's **Chain of Change**, but that work focuses on two later decades, the '60s and '70s. Similarly, the biographies of William Monroe Trotter open useful windows into Boston's Black community of the '20s and '30s, but they do not attempt to chart its political evolution.

Second, this history allows some of the city's senior Black activists to reflect — in their own words — on a critical and largely unappreciated period in the development of Black political culture in Boston. Is there a better way to know the character of a group of people than to discover how they view their own collective history?

This narrative is based in large part on oral history interviews with 25 prominent Black Bostonians, recorded on tape between July 1988 and February 1989. All who were interviewed are in a sense co-authors, whether or not they are quoted in the text. One anecdote, however insignificant, invariably led to another question, which led to more anecdotes — and, of course, more questions. Because I knew little or nothing about the subject of African-Americans and their politics in Boston when I began my research, everything I've written is borrowed — either from my own interviews, from published histories, from voting records, or from other oral history projects.

Various historical records notwithstanding, the past is much more than objective fact; its existence is primarily subjective — in individual and group consciousness. This narrative is an attempt to reconstruct the past by patching together individual memories and reflections like pieces of broken pottery. Such a reconstruction can be very useful, if we recognize its limits:

— There are going to be gaps.

If you repair a broken vase, some of whose shards have been lost, you don't expect it to hold water. This history is anything but definitive.

— Mistakes are possible.

Again, following the analogy of the reconstructed vase, the reader should bear in mind that in some instances pieces may be out of place

— even from another pot. I have tried to verify dates and other data, or find corroboration of two or more people, before using information. Nonetheless, much of the material from interviews and other sources could not be verified without painstaking research that would go far beyond the limitations of this project. Readers are advised to place more trust in the general contours of the past as outlined in this narrative than in any of the fascinating details that give it so much color and personality.

— Disagreement is healthy.

My interviews revealed significant disagreement both on facts and interpretation of historical events. Where I discovered disagreement, I have tried to treat each side fairly and allow the reader to decide what to believe.

Robert C. Hayden — well-known community historian, educator, and author — has developed a short curriculum guide for those interested in using this publication to introduce high school and college students to aspects of Boston's 20th-century Black history. The narrative should be a useful reference for libraries, scholars, and community activists. It is also hoped that this history will stimulate thought and discussion among Black Bostonians — not only about the past, but about contemporary political options. The issues of today, alas, are not so different from those of yesterday.

Finally, it should be more widely appreciated that the history of Boston's Black community is indispensable to an understanding of the city as a whole — and therefore of importance to each and every Bostonian.

Unless otherwise noted, all quotations are from interviews with those who participated in the recent oral history project. Some interviews not referred to in the narrative focus on events of the '60s and beyond. It is hoped that at least the decade of the '60s can someday be added to the narrative, something limited resources did not permit at this time.

The great value of such an undertaking is that it allows people to speak for themselves. And that — within limits imposed by providing sufficient background to make quotations meaningful — is what I have tried to do: let Black Bostonia speak for itself.

———

Chapter One

Atmospherics and Childhood Memories

When the United States declared itself at war with Germany in April of 1917, there were high hopes among African-Americans that their active participation in the war effort would remove a web of restrictive segregation laws spreading across the country.

Soon more than 2 million Blacks had registered for the draft, and students at Black colleges began to agitate for the commissioning of Black officers. By the fall of 1917 — although some Black leaders objected to a segregated facility — the National Association for the Advancement of Colored People (NAACP) had won a struggle with the Army for a special Officers Training School in Iowa for Black soldiers.

Madeline Kountze Dugger Kelley, who was born in Boston in 1897, recalls the battle of her husband, Edward Dugger, to become an officer:

"They wouldn't let him go to Plattsburg [to a regular Officers Training School]. They would not let Blacks in Plattsburg at the time. So they built anew. In Des Moines, Iowa, they built an Officers Training School just for Blacks, and he became a first lieutenant there...."

On October 15, 1917, Edward Dugger was one of 639 Black soldiers commissioned at Fort Des Moines. Nonetheless, high-ranking Army officers, even of segregated Black units, were uniformly white. The Marine Corps steadfastly refused to accept African-Americans at any rank.

When the war ended in 1919, the sweet taste of victory that swept most Americans optimistically into the 1920s quickly soured into bitter disappointment for Blacks, who were still generally deprived of voting rights in the South and still second-class citizens even in northern cities. In Boston, for instance, Edward Dugger and others had to fight after the war just to participate in the National Guard. Madeline Kountze Dugger Kelley — who would become a widow with six children in the '30s and Massachusetts Mother of the Year in 1952, the first African-American to be so honored — recalls the campaign to form the 372nd Infantry.

"He came back in 1918 [after fighting in Europe], and he was discharged. But they didn't have any outfits for Blacks then, so he had to wait a few years until they could get together and see if the government would let Blacks have the 372nd Infantry, which Blacks formed.... The most important thing was that we could not be recognized. So they, the men who enlisted, had to train for one whole year without pay, so we could have a Black outfit."

Peace brings violence

As discharged troops, Black and white, came home from Europe to compete for jobs, there was widespread racial violence. More than 70 Blacks were lynched within a year of the end of the war, and some 25 race riots broke out in American cities in 1919.

William Monroe Trotter — one of America's most radical civil rights leaders and publisher of Boston's foremost Black newspaper, *The Guardian* — tried to attend the Paris Peace Conference after WWI to petition for the rights of African-Americans. To prevent Trotter from raising the race issue at the peace talks, the U.S. State Department refused to issue him a passport for travel abroad. But nothing seemed to stop Trotter, once he set a course. Though delayed, he sailed to Europe as a ship's cook, using an assumed name and forged papers.

When Trotter arrived in Paris, President Woodrow Wilson and the rest of the official American delegation ignored his efforts to meet with them. After news reached Paris of a terrible lynching in Missouri, Trotter wrote the President an open letter, referring to the sacrifices of Black soldiers during the war:

"Will you not, therefore, for their sakes and that they shall not have died in vain, grant to their kin and race at home protection of right and life in the world peace agreement? And will you not at once send a special message to Congress, recommending that lynching be made a crime against the federal government?" Wilson took no action and made no reply.

Moving north

In part because of racial unrest in the South, the Black population of Boston was growing — from 16,350 in 1920 to 20,574 in 1930. Amanda Houston, a child of the '20s who would become prominent as a civic leader and educator in the '60s, describes her mother's decision to move from Florida to Boston at the end of the war:

"My mother [Alice Marie Samuels] migrated from Florida. She went to a school in Jacksonville, from which she was recruited [to come to Boston] by people who vacationed in and around the Florida area, who told her that Boston offered great opportunities for freedom and for expression."

Otto Snowden, who would found Freedom House in Roxbury in the '40s, came to Boston with his parents at the beginning of WWI, when he was about 3 years old. Prior to that, his father, who was just beginning an Army career, had been sent from Virginia to Delaware by the War Department. Delaware, Otto recalls, was a disappointment to his parents:

"He went to Wilmington, Delaware, but there was segregation there, and there was a one-room school [for Blacks]. So he asked to be transferred again, and he came to Boston..., where he finally retired as a Colonel, a full Colonel, after World War II."

Racial climate around Boston

Despite Boston's reputation for anti-slavery sentiments, Blacks who came north looking for a more sympathetic environment in "liberty's birthplace" soon discovered racial hostility beneath a thin veneer of courtesy and civility.

Otto Snowden's first vivid recollections of Boston came after his family moved to an apartment building at 63 Bainbridge Street in Roxbury, where Helen Whiteman, a retired school teacher from Washington, D.C., also lived:

"She was a Republican, as most of the Blacks were in those days. And she had a club. I cannot think of the name of the club right now, but it was one of the outstanding clubs in Boston. its major function was really politics....

"See, my father had a very very difficult time, because he was very bright, and working in the First Service Command here. The command would change every so often, and it got a Colonel in from the South who had said: 'Who is this Black man, head of a department?' He [Otto's father] was head of Personnel. And they demoted him. He went from top of the list to the bottom of the list about five times. And one guy, one Colonel, came in and said he didn't want a Black man working for him. So he had him transferred.... And Helen Whiteman was able to help him remain in Boston. And the Colonel came in shortly after that and said, 'Well, you beat me this time, but next time you're going to need the damn President to keep me from transferring you.'"

Amanda Houston's mother found work in the Boston suburb of Newton as a maid in the home of Alvan T. Fuller, Governor of Massachusetts from 1925 to 1929. As a result, she soon met Amanda's father, Harold Averett, chauffeur to another wealthy family. No one needed to explain Boston's racial problems to Averett; he had grown up a few miles north of Boston in West Medford, in the same integrated streets that had helped shelter Madeline Kountze from racial conflict — at least, she recalls, until she entered public school:

"You didn't get invited to any of the parties that the white children had. I remember I used to feel so bad, when I was 14 or 15 years old, when everybody would be going to parties and so forth and you never got invited.... Then it was very very segregated, very very prejudiced."

Madeline Kountze responded by pouring her prodigious energies into school work — and highjumping. She became the first girl ever to letter in sports at Medford High, and she won a scholarship to the Sergeant Normal School of Physical Training in Cambridge, where women learned to teach physical education.

"They didn't want to let me in [to the Sergeant School], because I was Black. Dr. [Dudley Allen] Sergeant was a great person. He said, 'I can't solve the race question. These girls are from the South, and they do not want to associate with Blacks. You're going to have a problem.' So the NAACP worked hard. We didn't get in until October; I should have gotten in in September. I couldn't go to camp or anything.... I felt so badly sometimes at the way I was treated, I would go downstairs and cry. No one ever saw me cry; I just went upstairs and beat them at everything they did, and that was that."

A career decision

Prejudice in northern cities could also produce violence, if not lynchings. While Madeline Kountze was at the Sergeant School, Henry Quarles Sr., who would become a prominent Black attorney in Boston, was making up his mind to study law:

"While I was a junior in high school, there was a man who was arrested for being concerned in promotion of the lottery, you know, the numbers game. And it was always illegal.... So over on Columbus Avenue there's a playground at Canton Street and Massachusetts Avenue, and it's called William E. Carter Playground. And this elderly colored man was arrested by the police and he became blind. They 'did a job on him' — for numbers! Two or three of the lawyers, the then-lawyers, in addition to Monroe Trotter, attempted to get complaints against the police officer in Boston Municipal Court without success.... And the entire neighborhood of the Black, or colored, people was concerned because they didn't get to first base in court. It was plain that this police officer ... received an increase in salary and in station — stature as a police officer. I think he was just an ordinary police officer; I think they made him a sergeant. I think his name was Long, as I recall now.

"So I was talking with my mother about it. And I said to my mother, 'I don't know what these lawyers talk about, but nothing will stop me from talking.... I wouldn't stand for no client taking that. I'm going to pursue law instead of engineering."

Quarles had been encouraged by teachers and counselors at Mechanic Arts High School in Boston to take a college preparatory course. But, he recalls, not many Blacks thought — or were thought of — in those terms:

"Most of the poor people, and most of the colored people in those days who attended that school, they did not take the college course. And they took a trade course, so they felt under the circumstances they could always get employment and so forth."

———

5

Progressive education

Elma Lewis, who would found and direct the Elma Lewis School of Fine Arts in Boston, was enrolled in a "progressive" nursery school program in 1924:

"I have my nursery school record. I was one of the first children in America who ever went to nursery school; it was an experimental movement.... I have a very impressive documentation of my nursery school experience, and it seems I enjoyed music, and I kept perfect rhythm, and I mimicked — and all of the things that show art talent were there. Interestingly enough, the PhD evaluating me, whom I assume was white, remarks that I came from a remarkable family — they will do anything they can to advance me — that I'm very gifted, in the arts particularly, and I have very fine verbal skills. And he concludes: 'But this bright, precocious little Negro girl will, as is usual for members of her race, test at a much lower level as she gets older. Train her to use her hands.'

"That is what has happened to Blacks in Boston — yes, in America. And if I had been from a less aggressive family, it would have happened to me.... I was 3 years and 11 months old, and the man had written me off!"

Were Black voices in Boston speaking out against such injustices? In the Boston of the 1920s, were there any Blacks in a position to stop them? Who were the political leaders? How were they organized? It is to such questions we now shall turn.

Chapter Two

The '20s

Forces in the Black Community

Black political activity in Boston was at low ebb during the early decades of the 20th century, suffering perhaps from a splintering of the solid African-American community that had established itself on Beacon Hill and in the West End during the 1800s. For decades, the Black community had been moving into the South End and lower Roxbury.

In his book *Chain of Change*, Mel King, who would become one of the most prominent Black politicians in Boston during the '60s, '70s, and '80s, attributes this political weakness to redistricting and displacement:

"... The Black community was able to elect two Black representatives in 1866 to the Massachusetts House of Representatives. As Republicans, Black representatives continued to be elected until 1896 when the districts were gerrymandered to make it impossible for the Black community to elect representatives. Also the housing on Beacon Hill at this time was being converted from wood to brick structures, in the process of which the Black community was relocated...."[1]

As the old community regrouped geographically, it also had to cope with a stream of newcomers from the South and the Caribbean, who intensified its cultural and political divisions. On the issue of race politics — how to respond to racial injustice and oppression — the energies of Black Bostonians were generally channeled into four related but often-conflicting fields: the separatist movement of Marcus Garvey, the National Association for the Advancement of Colored

People, the campaigns of William Monroe Trotter, and support for various politicians, most of them white.

This chapter explores each of these phenomena, and then analyzes the roles they played in a significant episode of the '20s: abandonment of all-Black Plymouth Hospital in favor of integration at Boston City Hospital.

Garveyism in Boston

Marcus Garvey, a native of Jamaica, began his protest movement there in 1914, brought it to Harlem with him in 1916, and saw it blossom after the First World War. His politics foreshadowed the Black power movement of the '60s and '70s. He was the first leader of the Black masses to preach the beauty of blackness. He said white Americans could never be converted from the racism they practiced and that Black Americans should flee to Africa to build a nation of their own. In 1921 he formed the African Republic, a kind of government-in-exile, and appointed himself Provisional President. He preached self-improvement, the development of Black enterprises, and separatism as opposed to integration. In all the larger American cities, millions of Garvey supporters attended weekly Universal Negro Improvement Association (UNIA) meetings.

Many prominent Bostonians of West Indian origin were raised on the teachings of Garvey. The Barbadian parents of Victor and John Bynoe, both of whom would be socially and politically prominent in Boston in coming decades, arrived in Boston about 1920. In 1928, Mrs. Bynoe returned to Barbados to pick up Victor and three sisters, who had been left behind in a grandmother's care. By this time, both parents were American citizens, and Mr. Bynoe was working as a carpenter on the New York Central Railroad. In 1928, when John was born, they were living on Windsor Street in the South End. Soon they would move to nearby Williams Street.

Here's how Victor describes his introduction to Boston's Garvey movement:

"At that time [1928], the Garvey movement was in full swing here. They [the Boston members] had bought a building at the corner of Walpole Street and Tremont Street [across from St. Cyprian's Episcopal Church], and they had a UNIA Hall. They had had many buildings before that, but that was the latest location. And the first Sunday of my arrival here, my father and my mother took me to the meeting. They had meetings on Sundays, Sunday evening at 4 o'clock. And there was the first time I got my introduction to the Garvey movement.... I was 14 years old.... Elma Lewis was there, the Clarks, the Griffiths. Oh, there were about a dozen young fellows like myself. They had formed a group of young men, who were the Cadets. The women were in uniform, and they had a men's corps — not too many....

"That was an every-Sunday proposition. You had to go because your parents took you. And, of course, it was the fundamentalist concept of nationalism — and Black this and Black that. And, of course, as you grew up, you got to understand what it was — a means of trying to inoculate the people into some sense of who they are and what they should be doing. We stayed there for years, until I got out of college, I think."

The parents of Ruth Batson, later a leader in the fight to desegregate Boston's public schools, were from Jamaica. She remembers the same UNIA meetings and her uncle serving as a Vice-President of the group.

Elma Lewis, whose nursery school experience we noted in the previous chapter, made her first stage appearance at a Garvey meeting as a three-year-old, reading a poem her father had found in the NAACP magazine, *The Crisis*. She says of her Barbados-born father:

"He was exceedingly political in the broadest sense of the word — not in the sense of being a Democrat or a Republican. The politics of race dominated his thinking, and I was raised to be a pan-African. He was a follower of Marcus Garvey, and we belonged all of our lives to the Universal Negro Improvement Association. Mother was a Black Cross nurse in that organization; he belonged to the African Legion. My brothers sold the *Negro World*, which was the newspaper, and I was a Girl Guide. The motto of Garvey was 'Up you mighty race, up you mighty people; you can what you will....'"

Here's how Elma Lewis describes Garvey's movement:

"Exceedingly strong. It was the strongest movement that Blacks have produced to date.... Somewhere between 1924 and 1926 — my dates may be a little fuzzy — ... Mr. Garvey had 4 million followers, who were Pullman porters and housemaids and janitors, who produced $6 million in revenue. I don't think that's been matched since, even now that we're more affluent.... Many of the things that you've seen since then — many of the concepts — came from that movement."

But, as a group, Garveyites ignored partisan politics, Victor Bynoe recalls:

"Didn't get involved at all. The Garvey movement did not take part in politics. Individuals in the Garvey movement might have, but the Garvey movement as a whole never subscribed or never attempted to get involved in politics. It [the movement in Boston] was not a large group. They were strictly West Indians and they were usually Barbadians and Jamaicans and a few others.... There were no outstanding leaders as far as the Garvey movement was concerned among the local group.... The intellectuals did not get involved in the Garvey movement. They were aloof... because I think they were concerned about the political opposition to the Garvey movement that was rampant. Because, you know, Garvey went to jail in '23 [for mail fraud], and the Republican Party really had it out to put him in jail, and they did. So... they [Boston's Garvey movement] didn't have enough strength to become a political entity.... If they had a hundred people at a meeting, it was plenty.... I suppose when I got here in '28, the thing had dropped off. In the early '20s — '23, before Garvey went to jail — I understand they used to be in places really crowded."

If meetings of the Garvey movement were attended primarily by West Indian immigrants, this didn't mean all West Indians were Garveyites or that the movement had no influence on others. Lucy Mitchell has noted that her husband, Joseph, who remained in Boston to become a prominent attorney, was so affected by the Garvey movement that he suggested — soon after her arrival in Boston in 1923 and not long after their marriage — that they leave the country to make a new life in Africa.[2] Lucy Mitchell would later become prominent for her efforts to improve day care institutions throughout Massachusetts.

William Monroe Trotter and the NAACP

In the political history of Boston's Black community, no name outshines Trotter's — not for what he accomplished, but for what he aspired to, not just for what he said and wrote, but for his dedication to the common cause. Trotter came into national prominence shortly after the turn of the century as the harshest Black critic of Booker T. Washington, undisputed leader of southern Blacks until his death in 1915. Washington was prepared to accept segregation and temporary second-class citizenship; Trotter, who was Harvard-educated, demanded full equality.

The Guardian, the newspaper Trotter founded in 1901, had a wide readership and attained national prominence because of its radical, unbending support for total desegregation at a time when Jim Crow laws enforced separation of the races in most of the country and discrimination was condoned almost everywhere.

How radical could Trotter be on the question of integration? Consider his opposition to the establishment of a Black hospital in 1908.

At the time, Black nurses and medical students could not train in Boston hospitals. As a partial remedy, Dr. Cornelius N. Garland converted a building on East Springfield Street into a hospital run for and by Blacks. Trotter criticized the venture in *The Guardian*. It would, he said, bring "far more ultimate harm in causing the Jim Crow laws to be drawn about us..." than benefits from jobs and training for Blacks.[3]

Despite Trotter's opposition, Garland was able to keep the hospital open, apparently with widespread support in the Black community. Trotter's career had peaked while he was in Paris in 1919, taking on Woodrow Wilson and the world single-handedly. Locally, his most provocative moments were a 1903 confrontation with Booker T. Washington at the A.M.E. Zion Church and his protest of the movie "The Birth of a Nation" in 1915. He couldn't stop Washington from speaking for the nation's African-Americans, or prevent the screening of D. W. Griffith's film, which portrayed Southern Blacks as depraved and glorified the Ku Klux Klan. But in opposition to them, he was courageously defiant.

Trotter helped organize the Boston Committee to Advance the Cause of the Negro in 1909. A year later, it became the first branch of the NAACP. Trotter even attended some early chapter meetings — but he never committed himself to the organization, which challenged his influence locally and nationally.

Trotter criticized the NAACP's relatively moderate stance on integration and the dominant role influential whites played in the organization. (In Boston, initially, the top three NAACP officers were white, and only two Blacks were on the six-member executive committee.) He was constantly at odds with W.E.B. DuBois, an acquaintance from Harvard and the only Black in the top ranks of the NAACP nationally.

—

11

As NAACP membership grew in the '20s, Trotter's own following waned. Both he and the NAACP sought support from successful Boston Blacks and from members of the old abolitionist Boston families. The NAACP offered them leadership opportunities; Trotter seldom shared power with anyone in the groups he headed — and certainly not with whites. His radical program, and particularly his combative behavior, made it difficult even for close friends to follow him. His inability to prevent the opening of Garland's hospital is indicative of the role he was forced to play — more the journalistic gadfly than the powerful leader of organized followers.

Trotter tried to speak for the Black masses in Boston, but with varied success; he was not one of them. Edward L. Cooper, who was 24 when he moved from Virginia to Boston in 1928, calls Trotter "a voice in the wilderness." In 1920, Trotter described his National Equal Rights League as "an organization of the colored people and for the colored people and led by the colored people." But a Trotter biographer refers to the NERL of the early '20s as "little more than a letterhead" on Trotter's stationery.[4] Victor Bynoe says of the NERL:

"It was not completely a Black organization. The Equal Rights League was one of these sophisticated organizations that dealt in the higher echelons and depended upon people of note to get involved. That, we just stayed away from it, because in our opinion we don't need the highfalutin folks to do this for us. Let us do it. We're the people that's starving; we need the jobs...."

One of those who was listening and following the "voice in the wilderness" was Rosa Brown. Mrs. Brown was an NERL member and mother-in-law and political mentor of Melnea Cass, who would become prominent in the Black politics of coming decades. Both would become active in the NAACP.

It is important to note the unifying role *The Guardian* and its rival, the *The Boston Chronicle* played in Massachusetts Black communities of the '20s and '30s. For instance, Mabray (Doc) Kountze, who was born in Medford in 1910, recalls the effect the *Guardian* had on Blacks in the Boston hinterlands, or what are now called suburbs:

"Everyone in the Black districts of Massachusetts knew the Boston *Guardian*. That was *the* paper, equal rights paper, and everyone knew about the *Guardian*. Some of us wrote ... articles for the Boston *Guardian* just for free, because we were so proud of our heritage. We would put in every marriage, every birth, every graduation and so on. And we all became a part of *The Guardian*."

What local issues was Trotter involved in during the '20s?

— He held an annual Boston Massacre Day celebration to honor Crispus Attucks, the Black who was the first in the fray to fall to British muskets.

— In 1921, he and the NAACP helped force the banning of "The Birth of a Nation," which had been scheduled for a rerun at the Shubert Theatre. There were 600 Blacks at Mayor Andrew Peters' public hearing on the film, which was held under a censorship law passed by the Legislature in 1915 in response to Black protests of the film's first Boston showing.

— In 1922, Trotter was one of many who successfully protested a decision by the President of Harvard University to exclude Black freshmen from college residence halls. He wrote in *The Guardian*, concerning his alma mater:

"If President Lowell is responsible for race exclusion in the freshman dormitory he is making Harvard turn from democracy and freedom to race oppression, prejudice and hypocrisy."

The local NAACP, by contrast, was reluctant to come to grips with local issues that could be divisive. A historical booklet published by the local branch[5] mentions the following:

— Investigation of cases of Black soldiers held at Fort Devens and forced to do menial labor long after they should have been discharged.

— Protests of lynching and support of anti-lynching legislation.

— Refutation of charges that the NAACP was being used by Communists.

— Assistance to Blacks denied access to the ballot (presumably in other parts of the country).

— Fighting against housing and job discrimination.

It is noteworthy that none of these campaigns focuses on anything specific to Boston. Concern over brutal oppression of Southern Blacks, as opposed to perhaps equally debilitating if subtle racism at home, is perhaps understandable. But it must have bothered Trotter.

Electoral politics

As the constant influx of needy families far exceeded the means of Black churches and settlement houses to help them, whatever jobs, services, and influence could be wrested from local government were sorely needed. Both the NAACP and the Garvey movement steered clear of party politics — and *The Guardian* left Trotter little time to organize locally. Therefore, most day-to-day political activity fell to a group of part-time politicians, few of whom held public office.

The election of Blacks in Boston seemed almost out of the question. During the '20s, the city's Black population grew about six times as fast as the white population,[6] but the added numbers did not translate into political clout, in part because of difficulty in assimilating the newcomers into the community. Even in 1929 the black population of the city was still less than 3 percent of the total — about 20,000 in a city of more than 780,000.

Myrtle Worthy, daughter of Dr. William Worthy, recalls her father supporting two Black candidates, Dr. Andrew Lattimore and Attorney Matthew Bullock, in campaigns for the State House in 1920. Both were Republicans; neither was successful. It is noteworthy that Dr. Worthy was not again active in electoral politics until 1928, when he backed two white Democrats, Al Smith for president and David Walsh for the U.S. Senate.

Dr. Worthy's conversion to the Democratic Party brought him into collaboration with the controversial, if legendary, Silas (Shag) Taylor. The two probably had a professional association before they became political allies, as Taylor was the owner of the Lincoln Pharmacy on Tremont Street in lower Roxbury, not far from Worthy's South End medical office.

Taylor rose to prominence on the coattails of James Michael Curley, the powerful Congressman, Mayor, and Governor who several times ran afoul of the law, serving prison terms both early and late in his colorful career. Silas Taylor was never legally indicted, much less convicted of any wrongdoing, but charges that he used his political connections to run an after-hours saloon are so frequently recalled that they are hard to discount, reflecting as they do the political ethics of many Boston politicians in the '20s, when votes were routinely bought and sold.

For many in the Black community, the question of what Taylor and his brother, Balcom, were able to do for themselves was of less significance than what they were able to do for others. Ed Cooper recalls Shag Taylor as "a good politician":

"I knew Shag Taylor very well.... Shag would do anything for anybody within the framework of what he could do.... He was the man — the Black person — closest to James Michael Curley. And although Shag won't go down in history as having caused 15 or 20 people to get jobs under Curley, Shag did a lot of little favors for people, the same way Curley did a lot of little favors for Irish people."

Madeline Kountze Dugger Kelley recalls of Taylor:

"Shag Taylor was a very great person. He was an all-around politician and ... he was a citizen of the people and for the people.... Michael Curley and Shag Taylor worked together to do what they could in those days with the segregation what it was...."

On the other hand, Amanda Houston says her mother had such a low opinion of Silas Taylor that she would not have thought of approaching him for help. Nonetheless, she did not hesitate to turn to Curley:

"My mother used to very literally go and sit outside of Curley's door," Amanda recalls.

Myrtle Worthy recalls Shag Taylor and her father founding a political group in the late '20s:

"My father; and Dr. Walter O. Taylor; and Dr. Silas Taylor, the druggist; and Julian Rainey, the attorney; they formed a club, the Massachusetts Colored Men's Democratic Club. And shortly after that, they asked my mother to open a women's auxiliary, which she did. But after a while, the women wanted to be independent, so they formed the Massachusetts Colored Women's Democratic Club."

This faction supported Al Smith for president in 1928 and James Michael Curley in his successful bid for reelection as Mayor of Boston in 1929. In general, Shag Taylor would dominate the Democratic Party in Wards 9 and 12 until his death in the 1950s.

Of course, throughout the '20s most Blacks were still Republican, loyal to the "Party of Lincoln." But the tide had begun to turn. Irish Democrats were in political control of the city, and loyalty to the GOP was not meeting the needs of a struggling community, as Henry Quarles Sr. recalls:

"The colored folks ... figured that the Republicans 'ain't gettin' us nowhere.' Then colored people began thinking this is our life now, we can go and become Democrats — and they did with success."

If Curley had no special affection for Blacks, his heartfelt sympathy for the poor was apparently universal. Curley provoked the ire of the entire African-American community in 1915, when he allowed the showing of "The Birth of a Nation," despite Black protests. By the mid-'20s, however, he was apparently forgiven by most.

Even Victor Bynoe, who tried repeatedly to defeat Curley in the '30s and '40s, had little antipathy for him personally:

"I thought he was an affable guy. My whole argument against him was that he had picked this fellow Shag Taylor as his Black representative, and Shag Taylor was no person, in my opinion, to be a leader of the colored people."

Bynoe says white Democrats of the Curley era preferred to work with Taylor, rather than other Black Democrats, because "they knew him for what he was, and you didn't have to give him too much.....

"When I first came around Boston, politics election day was done this way: Shag Taylor would be the representative of the people that are in. And we were trying to put in somebody else, so we really had a tough battle. And they would come up and give him anything he wanted. They would give him liquor; they'd give him anything. And he was the dispenser of goodies. And so, if you didn't have anything to give, you got nothing."

Plymouth Hospital, an episode

The 1908 opening of a Black hospital by Dr. Garland, over the objection of William Monroe Trotter, has already been mentioned. In the mid-'20s, Myrtle Worthy recalls, Plymouth Hospital was shut down:

"It was closed because of financial reasons in 1925. Then two years later he [Dr. Garland] wanted to open up the new Plymouth Hospital, and it was to be a bigger hospital, and they meant it to be a hospital for colored. And it would mean eventually that the colored would be shut out of the City Hospital and the clinics and sent there to the hospital. That was when my father and Dr. Walter O. Taylor and some others opposed it. And Mr. Trotter of *The Guardian* opposed it — a segregated hospital in Boston."

Once again, Trotter attacked Garland's hospital plans in *The Guardian*, setting off a bitter dispute in 1928. Trotter feared that Boston was tottering on the brink of Southern-style segregation.

Where were the other sectors of the Black community in this debate?

—

16

It is likely that the prospect of a large Black-run hospital appealed to the Garveyites, whose Black nationalism specifically called for separatist Black-owned businesses and institutions. But the group took no stand. As individuals, however, they probably supported hospital expansion, even if many who supported Dr. Garland's hospital also hoped to see Boston's teaching hospitals admit Black nurses and interns.

Although they favored gradual steps toward integration, Boston's NAACP leadership tried to avoid issues like Plymouth Hospital expansion that were sure to shatter solidarity in the local chapter. When the hospital issue became divisive, a prominent white member of Garland's biracial expansion committee, Moorefield Storey, resigned in the heat of Trotter's attack on Garland's plan. Storey (who lived in Lincoln, a fashionable suburb of Boston) had served as the first President of the Boston NAACP Chapter. His resignation indicated which way the winds were blowing.

Led by two Black doctors, W. O. Taylor and William Worthy, a committee of citizens, including Trotter and his sister Maude Steward, championed the cause of two local Black girls, recent graduates of Cambridge High and Latin School who applied for admission to the nursing program at Boston City Hospital in 1929. The hospital interviewed them and then ignored their applications. The members of the committee reasoned that if these girls could gain admission to the nurses training program at City Hospital, support for a separate hospital to serve Black Bostonians would collapse. "As taxpaying citizens," Dr. Worthy wrote in one of a number of letters from the committee to the hospital authorities, ... "we are insisting on their legal rights to the same treatment accorded others in a 'School' supported by public taxes."[7]

After months of effort on the part of the committee, the hospital Trustees yielded and City Hospital admitted the Black students. Some say James Michael Curley deserves credit for breaking the impasse, but Dr. Worthy writes that "... no politician had anything whatsoever to do with this transaction."[8] In his history of Medford's Black community, Mabray (Doc) Kountze quotes Harriet Blanchard Darden, formerly a nurse at Plymouth hospital, reminiscing about its closing:

"I knew of not one Colored nurse in a white hospital. That didn't even begin to happen until the 1920s, when Mayor Michael J. Curley [sic] issued an ultimatum for the Boston City Hospital to hire Colored.

The City Hospital head, a woman, refused — and said she would quit if Colored nurses and doctors were admitted. Curley let her go, and Colored entered City Hospital and other Boston hospitals thereafter.... There was now no need for a Boston Colored hospital...."[9]

The fact that Curley was not mayor of Boston in 1929 suggests that we may be dealing here with some folklore that credited the colorful Curley with more than he achieved. On the other hand, Curley was already the victor in the all-important Democratic mayoral primary in the spring of 1929 before the Trustees' decision. He could have made his views known to officials at the hospital, which he would control after his inauguration.

Two years later, when the first Black intern was finally accepted for training at City Hospital, Curley was Mayor and at least in touch with hospital officials about the issue. Dr. Worthy tells of calling on the President of the hospital, Joseph Manning, on behalf of the Black applicant, John B. Hall:

"He also told me that Mayor James M. Curley had called him to inquire about John's status, but that he had made no requests or suggestions about him. No doubt, Mayor Curley's interest in this case was helpful to the Committee, but he was not responsible for John's appointment, as has been claimed."[10]

Both Dr. Worthy and Dr. Taylor were associated with Plymouth Hospital before it closed in 1925 and were charter members with Shag Taylor of the Massachusetts Democratic Colored Men's Club at about the time the hospital tried to reopen and expand. All three were probably deeply involved in Curley's 1929 reelection campaign. If there is no convincing evidence that Curley was part of the initial integration of City Hospital, there is also no indication he tried to prevent it — as he prevented the banning of "The Birth of a Nation" in 1915.

Whether Curley did or did not play a role in the hospital incident, it is worth noting that by the end of the '20s, Shag Taylor, Dr. Worthy, and other Black Democrats were in a position to influence the pugnacious Irishman on such issues — something Trotter and the NAACP were not positioned to do in 1915.

Chapter Three

The '30s

Jobs, Jobs, Jobs!

A job — or lack of a job — had been a central factor in the lives of most Black families since emancipation. But in the 1930s — in the face of widespread economic depression — the search for jobs preoccupied the entire community.

As a consequence, the political event of the '30s in Boston's Black community was the gravitation of its voters to the Democratic Party. The Democrats promised jobs. The shift to the Democrats didn't mean that party labels were of vital concern to Black voters — they weren't. It didn't mean that by 1940 there weren't still a lot Black Republicans — there were. It meant that Black voters, stirred by the challenge of the Depression years, were increasingly independent and responsive to the specific programs of political candidates.

If there were no electoral victories to celebrate in the '30s, it was not because the community was disorganized or politically inactive — its votes were simply too few to elect Black candidates. Allan Rohan Crite, whose paintings chronicle life in Boston's South End, was a student at the Museum School from 1930 to 1937. He recalls community protests of discriminatory hiring practices:

"Serving as a clerk in a store was practically a 'no-no.' And, of course, there were strong movements ... 'Don't buy where you can't work.' And so, I remember ... quite a few demonstrations."

Boycotts and street protests of job discrimination did not change Boston employment patterns in the '30s, but the political aspirations of the Depression years set the stage for significant victories after World War II.

Climbing in Roxbury

The 1930s completed a consolidation of the Black community in the South End and Roxbury. When Charles Street Church, the last Black institution on Beacon Hill, moved to the corner of Warren Street and Elm Hill Avenue in Roxbury in 1939, it symbolized the end of an era. The church was simply following the vanguard of pioneering middle-class Blacks up what was sometimes called "Sugar Hill" — in reference to an exclusive section of Harlem — toward Franklin Park and the higher elevations of Roxbury.

The Rev. Michael Haynes, who would represent Boston at the State House and become pastor of Twelfth Baptist Church, grew up in lower Roxbury during the '30s. Here are some of his earliest memories:

"At that time, I was living on Haskins Street. And Ruggles Street, when I was growing up, was sort of the line. Blacks were just beginning to move across that line of Ruggles Street. There were already Blacks living in the Humbolt Avenue area.... But moving up a little higher, you had a scattering of Blacks who might have been at that time, in the early '30s, the bourgeois, the Black bourgeois, in the Boston area, because there were a number of lawyers and doctors who were living in that area....

"There were several apartment houses on my street that were changing from Jewish to Black. And a lot of the private homes, the single homes, were changing from ... white Protestant and Catholic to Black."

Republicans become "special"

Haynes also remembers a neighbor on Haskins Street named Mrs. Myrick, a hairdresser whose eldest daughter opened her own business at the corner of Cabot and Ruggles:

"As time went on, she had a husband, and he seemed to be important. I can see him now. He was the first person that I heard talk of: 'He was a Republican.' That was supposed to be something very big and something very important."

The man's name was Wilfred Scott, and Haynes also says of Scott that he was "fortunate to be a Republican," which was "supposed to be something special."

Republicans, who were hard to find on Haskins Street, were more likely to live in upper Roxbury, on and off Humbolt Avenue. These more comfortably situated Black families were less likely to join the populist Democratic Party of James Michael Curley and Franklin D. Roosevelt, although there were significant exceptions — Dr. Worthy, for one.

But Wilfred Scott was "something special" even among Republicans, because Scott, who was a heavy contributor to the Republican Party, had a number of influential friends. Haynes recalls his older brothers talking about going to "Mr. Scott" for help in finding jobs.

Fighting poverty

Melnea Cass and her husband, Marshall, moved to Roxbury from the South End in 1930. He was soon among the jobless, losing his position as a technician in a dental laboratory. Mrs. Cass became a live-in housekeeper to keep the family fed and sheltered. Until Marshall found work with the General Services Administration, much of the care of their children fell to Rosa Brown, Marshall's mother.

Victor Bynoe says of Mrs. Cass, who would become one of Boston's most dynamic Black leaders and "First Lady of Roxbury," that in these early days she was relatively subdued, because "she had a mother-in-law who ran her whole life for her." Mrs. Cass was Vice-President of the Harriet Tubman Mother's Club. It was named after one of the most successful leaders of the Underground Railroad and its members tried to "mother" young women who had just arrived in Boston from the South. She was Secretary of a similar club, the Sojourner Truth Club, named after the Black abolitionist and suffragist. Her mother-in-law was President of the Sojourner Truth group.[11]

There was, of course, much work to be done by such civic-minded groups. If there was a growing Black middle class on "Sugar Hill" in the '30s, it was not growing as fast as the ranks of the destitute on certain drab streets in the South End and lower Roxbury, where some victims of the Depression paid $10 a month to huddle in unheated wooden tenements. Some of the truly down and out built ragged shacks near the dump on Mile End Road.

Rampaging patronage

The practice of rewarding loyal political supporters by putting them or their friends on the public payroll was practiced in Boston long before the '30s. But, as the ranks of the unemployed and the number of persons working for government rose dramatically during the Depression, politics in Boston became virtually synonymous with patronage. In 1934, 33.9 percent of the Black work force was unemployed. The figure fell to 30.3 percent by 1940 — when 8.5 percent were working on government projects.[12] Anyone controlling government jobs was in a position to do significant "favors."

It is estimated that in 1940 Black workers held about 13 percent fewer jobs than was their "fair share" on government work projects. This compares unfavorably with Irish laborers, who secured 14 percent more than their proportional share — but it compares quite favorably with Italian laborers, who filled about 40 percent fewer of these jobs than their numbers indicate they should have.[13]

Ed Cooper refers to Wilfred Scott, the Republican Michael Haynes thought was so special, as "the Republican counterpart" of Shag Taylor:

"Those guys did a lot of favors for a lot of Black people.... Wilfred Scott was the kind of politician who worked behind the scenes. Everybody knew that Shag had connections with James Michael Curley. And Shag was more out in the open. But Wilfred Scott was the kind of person who would pick up the telephone and call some of his Republican friends — [Leverett] Saltonstall, for instance — and get Saltonstall [Governor from 1939 to 1945] to do favors for you.... He [Scott] was very influential in those years."

Victor Bynoe calls Scott a "gentleman politician":

"He was personally wealthy in his own right. He wasn't selling booze after hours. That was the thing that I couldn't see about Shag; that was a disgrace."

Just how much Scott could help his Republican friends at election time is not clear. Nonetheless, as the Black vote in Wards 9 and 12 grew, far-sighted Republicans kept up their ties to influential Black families — ties that would pay the party handsome dividends in the electoral victories of Edward Brooke in the 1960s.

The Black population of Boston only increased by about 15 percent during the '30s, down considerably from its 26 percent growth rate in the '20s.[14] But there was an impressive gain in the strength of the Black vote in the two Black wards, particularly among Democrats.

Party membership was often a matter of "favors." Otto Snowden recalls how he became a Republican in the mid-'30s:

"I turned a Republican when I was 21 years old.... My father, who was somebody active in politics, had me go to one of the Black politicians, whom I will not name, to tell about this job that I wanted.... So he [the Black politician] says: Was I registered? I said, 'Yes, as an Independent.' He said, 'Well, you turn a Republican — you know, sign up as a Republican — and I'll go to bat for you.' Which I did. But I didn't get the job."

Traditional political jobs for Blacks

Of course, influential Blacks were not always catered to by their white Republican friends. Ed Cooper has not forgotten how the party treated one of the more prominent Black Republicans of the day:

"There was a man who lived in lower Roxbury by the name of Matthew W. Bullock. He's dead now. And Mr. Bullock decided to run for the City Council, because we had a guy in the City Council by the name of Flynn, I believe, who had been on the City Council for quite a few years, and lower Roxbury was beginning to become more Black as the years progressed. And I think it was probably in 1934 or 1935 that Matthew W. Bullock decided that he might want to run for the City Council. He was Black, a Black lawyer and ... Republican. People downtown decided that they would take Matt Bullock out of the race for City Council and they would appoint him to the Parole Board — as an attempt, in my opinion, to prevent Blacks from getting into the political arena."

Venturing into electoral politics was risky for Blacks in the '30s. If white Republicans would not support him enthusiastically, Bullock was probably wise to take the Parole Board seat, which would become a traditional Black appointment.

Victor Bynoe says of Bullock:

"That they never took care of him was one of the tragedies of the Republican Party.... He was the guy who was cast aside in those days. In Depression days, they put him on the Parole Board.... He was a gentleman; he was a real credit to the colored people.... When he left, they sent Shag up there [to the Parole Board], and they reorganized the Parole Board to get him [Shag] out of there. It was one of those things that was unfortunate."

When Julian Rainey, attorney and close associate of Shag Taylor, was appointed Assistant Corporation Counsel for the City of Boston by Mayor Curley, there were apparently only two other Blacks in significant government positions: Bullock, who was on the Parole Board, and William L. Reed. Reed was appointed Executive Secretary of the Governor's Council in 1924 and remained in the office under both Republican and Democratic Governors until 1942.

Of the three, Rainey appears to have been most active during the '30s. Victor Bynoe, who continually fought with Shag Taylor, seems even less enamored of Rainey than of Taylor.

"He was very easily swayed.... He was Assistant District Attorney under Curley and their [Assistant] Corporation Counsel, but he was the kind of guy you couldn't be sure of.... So we young guys lost faith in Julian."

Perhaps part of the disenchantment with Rainey was the fact that he often sought jobs from those he supported for election, unlike Shag Taylor, Dr. Worthy, or Wilfred Scott — all relatively well-to-do.

Bullock and Reed represented the deep Republican roots in the Black community. By all accounts a consummate politician, Reed was a Ward 9 Committeeman in 1887, when the ward was still on Beacon Hill. He was Deputy Internal Revenue Collector for the City of Boston before the turn of the century and was appointed Executive Messenger and Clerk to Governor W. Murray Crane in 1902, a position he held for many years.[15]

Reed is not, however, remembered as a great leader of the Black community of the '20s and '30s. Perhaps the difficulty of holding down a State House position through successive administrations prevented him from taking a vigorous role in community politics. In any case, the relative weakness of Blacks as a voting bloc forced Reed, Bullock, and Rainey to depend on the goodwill of white politicians for the positions they held. That they probably performed their jobs well is evident from the long-observed tradition of appointing Blacks to offices they were the first to fill: Executive Secretary of the Governor's Council, Assistant Corporation Counsel for the City of Boston, and state Parole Board member.

Joseph S. Mitchell ('43-'44), Bruce Robinson ('47-'48), Clarence Elam ('53-'56), and Elwood McKinney ('57-'60) all served as Secretary to the Governor's Council. The position was particularly appealing because it could serve as a springboard for appointment to other state offices. Robinson and McKinney would leave the Executive Council to become judges in '48 and '60 respectively. Elam, whose brother Harry would also become a judge, was appointed Chairman of the Boston Licensing Board when he left the council in '56.

Ed Cooper recalls Robinson's historic appointment:

"Governor Bradford appointed Judge Bruce Robinson as ... an Associate Justice of the Boston Juvenile Court — the first Black Judge that had been appointed since the 1880s...."

The negative side of such traditional offices as Secretary to the Governor's Council was that, as time went by, the Black community could waste undue energy on simply keeping Blacks in these positions — and especially on deciding who would fill them — Otto Snowden recalls:

"What used to disturb me — the Blacks would fight. And the Republicans would then say, 'Remove the Black Democrat, and put me in.' ... 'Let's ask for some more, something new.' That was my philosophy."

Ed Cooper comments:

"I remember when ... [Robert] Bradford was Governor [1947-49]. Someone running for political office during that time mentioned the Executive Secretary of the Governor's Council. And I took the position then, and I still take that position, that if the governor, instead of appointing a Black as Executive Secretary to the Governor's Council, would appoint 10 or 15 secretaries, which would give more opportunity for Blacks than just having one as Exhibit A, then Blacks in this state would be better [served].... They finally did away with having a Black in the Executive Secretary of the Governor's Council. And in my opinion, it was a good thing, because it opened up additional opportunities for Blacks in other state agencies."

Henry Quarles Sr. recalls eminent Boston attorney William H. Lewis asking him to represent a man who was related by marriage to Lewis's sister — and who was arrested at the State House in 1929, the year the stock market crashed:

"In 1929, his [Lewis's] sister in Cambridge had ... an in-law, and ... he was arrested at the State House. He had taken an examination for a job, and they did not appoint him. He maintained that he came out the highest of any of the persons who took the examination.... So he got his gun and went to the State House to see them, I guess. And he shot him [someone at the State House] in the ear and they arrested him and they charged him with being an insane person.... And Mr. Lewis contacted me to represent him...."

Curley's influence noted

Nationwide, the Democratic gains of the '30s might simply reflect a devastated economy, a Republican tendency to woo white Southerners, and the popularity of Franklin D. Roosevelt. But in Boston, the personal appeal of James Michael Curley was an additional factor. True, Curley did not win the hearts of the Black community when he refused to ban "The Birth of a Nation" in 1915 during his first term as Mayor. But by the end of the '20s, as previously noted, Curley enjoyed the very active support of Dr. William Worthy, Shag Taylor, and Julian Rainey. And they, in turn, could expect favors from Curley and those he appointed while Mayor (1930-33) and Governor (1935-37).

The extent of Curley's influence is reflected in the support Blacks in Boston gave Franklin D. Roosevelt in 1932 — an estimated 65 percent of their votes.[16] Blacks in most of the country did not jump onto the Roosevelt bandwagon until the election of 1936. For instance, only about 23 percent of Chicago's Black vote supported the Democratic ticket in 1932.[17] In Boston, the Black vote for Roosevelt stayed high through the 1940 election — 64 percent in 1936, 67 percent in 1940 — despite the fact that an African-American, James W. Ford, was vice-presidential candidate on the Communist Party ticket in '32, '36, and '40. No wonder Julian Rainey ranked high among African-Americans advising national leaders of the Democratic Party during the Roosevelt years.[18]

From 1928 to 1940, the three radical parties of the left (Socialist, Socialist Labor, and Communist) only once captured more than 2,000 presidential votes in Boston — 7,091 votes in 1932.[19] The vote for the radical left in 1932 was not large (Boston's population was about 780,000), but it showed that class politics made significant gains during the early '30s, before Roosevelt's New Deal programs began to help those hardest hit by the Depression.

There was some organized Black opposition to Curley and his Black Democratic supporters in the '30s, even among Democrats. For instance, Victor Bynoe, just out of college, was Democrat Maurice Tobin's campaign manager in the Black community when Tobin defeated Curley to become Mayor in 1937.

Even after Tobin's victory, however, Shag Taylor and his co-workers were not without influence in City Hall, Bynoe recalls:

"... Shag Taylor and them had a way of getting around to him [Tobin].... Of course, you couldn't convince the youngsters that, look, this is the beginning, until you were able to give them something. And there wasn't enough to give anybody."

By 1946, Curley had regained City Hall, and "Shag was back in the roost again," Bynoe adds. "We didn't get another shot until we elected Hynes [in '49]...."

Police, firemen, teachers

Of course, one reason the Depression was particularly devastating for Blacks was the fact that they were not even considered for many jobs — even in the public sector.

Both the NAACP and the Urban League spoke out vigorously against federal job training programs that refused to prepare Blacks for anything but household work. George Goodman, Executive Secretary of the Urban League in Boston, issued a prophetic warning to the Works Progress Administration that, if Blacks were not trained for more dignified employment, "there will be ... problems that we cannot now see."[20]

Ed Cooper notes that after the 1919 police strike there wasn't another Black placed on the Boston Police Force till the middle of World War II:

"Between 1919 and 1943, there wasn't a Black police officer appointed to the Boston Police Department. And when I hear people today talking about discrimination, and I look at the paucity of Black policemen on the Boston Police Force from 1919 to 1943 — if we had done the right thing in those years: one, we would have more Blacks on the Police Force and, two, we wouldn't have all this hullabaloo about affirmative action and discrimination against whites.

"In the same connection, between 1928, when I came here, and 1943, there was one Black fireman on the Boston Fire Department.

There was a paucity of Blacks in the public school system. I remember in 1928 — between 1928 and 1933 — there wasn't a teacher appointed to the Charlestown High School, because a Black girl by the name of Campbell was at the head of the list, and they didn't want to put Campbell on, so they didn't appoint a teacher to the Charlestown High School for five years. Finally they had to appoint ... this Black girl as teacher."

First public housing project

The 1930s saw the first public housing project built in Boston. Ed Cooper recalls the development of the projects:

"I remember in 1937 when the Boston Housing Authority built Old Colony in South Boston.... Old Colony was the first housing development built in the United States under public housing. Old Colony was built and called — and is still called — a 'white' project. In 1938, Lenox Street was built, and Lenox Street was called then the 'colored' project — and is still an all-Black project.... And when I think in terms of what is happening in terms of housing today — the NAACP is suing the Boston Housing Authority — as with the Police Department, as with the teachers, the teaching system, if the Boston Housing Authority had had the foresight in 1937 to do the right thing by part of its citizens, instead of having a 'white' project and a 'colored' project, ... Mayor Flynn wouldn't be scratching his head where it doesn't itch."

Would public pressure on the Housing Authority have made a difference? Where was the pressure to come from? Not from William Monroe Trotter. On his 60th birthday, April 6, 1934, Trotter apparently took his own life, perhaps in despair over the state of his newspaper, which was near bankruptcy.

Historian Lerone Bennett Jr. would later write:

"A true pioneer, decades ahead of his time, Trotter laid the first stone of the modern protest movement." [21]

The NAACP in the '30s

A history of the Boston branch written by former NAACP Branch President Robert C. Hayden lists the following branch initiatives for the first half of the decade:

"1930 — Butler Wilson, Branch President, presided at a Memorial service for Moorfield Storey at the Park Street Church.

"1931 — William Pickens, the national field secretary of the NAACP, addressed a mass meeting of the Branch on the 'Scottsboro' case involving nine black youths charged with rape in Alabama.

"1933 — Roy Wilkins was the keynote speaker at the Annual Meeting held at the 20th Century Club on Joy Street."

Now notice how much more vital are the entries for second half of the '30s:

"1936 — Black attorney Irwin Dorch became the third President of the Branch; a goal of 5,000 members was set. Five hundred new members were gained. Dues were $1.00.

"The '30s brought the establishment of the Branch's first formal youth activity. In 1936 a Youth Council was organized with 58 members from 25 different community youth groups and churches.

"1937 — The Boston Branch Youth Council held a mass meeting against educational inequality in the schools.

"— The Branch sent out letters protesting discrimination; in the rates charged and the employment practices of insurance companies, and employment discrimination by public utility companies. Metropolitan Insurance Co. replied that 'They do not hire colored people as agents or secretaries — but that they do not refuse to issue ordinary policies merely because of color.' No replies were received from John Hancock Insurance Co., Boston Consolidated Gas Co., or the Boston Edison Company.

"1938 — The Branch filed a bill to prohibit public utility corporations from refusing employment on account of race.

"— Branch protested to the Police Department about officers breaking into homes of 'colored' citizens at late hours without a search warrant or reason.

"— Branch fought and won an extradition case against Eugene Wilson, who was apprehended in Boston as a fugitive from a Georgia chain gang. The publicity around this case moved the Georgia legislature to abolish the chain gang system."[23]

Note how much more local and specific are the protests of the '30s, compared with those of the '20s. There has been an infusion of new blood and vitality; it is the Youth Council of the chapter that registers a prophetic protest over inequality in the schools. There is, however, as yet no mention of segregation in public housing.

While a college student in the '30s, Victor Bynoe was one of the "youngsters" that went to the churches to broaden NAACP membership. He says of the local branch:

"The NAACP was a parlor discussion group in the early days—too long.... The NAACP never became effective until it got down to the little people."

Amanda Houston notes that her family never had much confidence in the NAACP locally:

"We [as a family] never supported the NAACP in Boston — the NAACP as practiced in this city, which is a different NAACP. There have been times when the national NAACP has talked of snatching the charter here — the NAACP here is so reactionary."

Coping with the Depression

After Amanda Houston's father died in 1931, her mother took a live-in job as cook and maid in suburban Newton. About five years later, she married Paul Green, a Hampton College graduate from Norfolk, Virginia. Green started out as a salesman for American Supply on Washington Street. During the '30s he was laid off and forced to work for the Works Progress Administration (WPA) collecting garbage, much to his chagrin. Green would soon become a redcap at Back Bay Station, and then open up a real estate office, where Royal Bolling Sr. would eventually work.

In the late '30s, Bolling, who would enjoy a long career representing Boston in the state legislature, was just getting his first taste of electoral politics as candidate for senior class president at suburban Framingham High School West of Boston:

"At that time a former Mayor of Boston, Mayor Curley, was

running for governor. And his opponent, Republican opponent, was Leverett Saltonstall. And so I wrote a letter to each of them, telling them that I was running for president of my class, and I would appreciate some letter of encouragement. And so it just happened that both answers came on the same day. And they praised me for being involved in the school politics, and went on to say what their goals were in Massachusetts, etc. So immediately, I had the letters blown up and big signs made, saying that Curley and Saltonstall had endorsed me for class president!"

Bolling, whose letters to Curley and Saltonstall did not identify him as one of only four Blacks at Framingham High School, won the class election. Perhaps, at the time he wrote the letters, race seemed irrelevant to Bolling; he had experienced relatively few racial incidents in the Framingham schools. When he tried to find a job after graduation, however, the significance of race became crystal clear:

"When I graduated from high school [in 1939], I had taken a college course, with no idea of ever being able to go to college. And it was traditional that the president of the graduating class could always get a job at the Dennison Manufacturing Company, which was a big manufacturing company in Framingham and in Massachusetts. And so I went to the personnel office, and the head of personnel was the father of one of my classmates. And so he just came right out and he said: "I'm not going to beat around the bush with you or anything.... It's a policy of this company not to hire colored people.' And he turned and went in."

Working as a gardener in nearby Wellesley helped convince Bolling that he should go to college — if he could somehow find a way to pay for it:

"I had learned how to tap dance at a school in Framingham. The teacher, incidentally, was a white fellow from New Hampshire.... But over the years I became proficient ... and I met various other young people who had various talents, etc. So I got in touch with them and asked them if they would be in a show with me that I was going to produce in Framingham to raise money to go to college. And they, without exception, agreed to do it. And then my high school classmates sold the tickets, etc., and I had already applied for Howard University in Washington, D. C., and had been accepted. So we put on the show. We had a great show, and I had enough money for the first year's tuition [about $800]."

Bolling wasn't the only Black youth who used artistic talent to help pay college expenses during the Depression. Elma Lewis began her performance career much earlier:

"All of my life, the people in the Black community supported me beautifully. I have been earning my living since I was 11 years old. When I was a little girl, I used to read poetry on stages. And I would read from the works of Tennyson, I would read Shakespeare — I would read all of those people. And a section of the program was always Langston Hughes, James Weldon Johnson, and the Black authors — Paul Laurence Dunbar. On Sunday afternoon, I would go to two churches. They would have what you call musical teas and concerts. And they would pay me $15 apiece. They sold tickets for a dollar apiece, and they'd have 200 to 300 people. And they'd have a singer and a reader, or a pianist and a singer — or whatever.... Now in the middle of the week, on Thursday, I went to a church in the white community and made $20. I was making $50 a week when my father was making $11. I made enough money to go through college and graduate school."

Campus tales

Madeline Kountze Dugger Kelley's son, Edward Jr., was an outstanding member of the track team at Tufts College in Medford:

"Eddie, my eldest son, was captain of the track team at Medford High School, and then he was also captain of his track team at Tufts College. Up here at Tufts College, the men were his own friends and he didn't have too many problems. It was only when he went out to run in some place like Texas, where he couldn't stay in a hotel with the rest of them [that he had problems].... His friends always stood by him, but he had a lot of terrible experiences. In fact, when he went to run at Princeton once, the coach said, 'Well, you go with him.... Take my ticket.' I went with him. As soon as we got near New Jersey, the taxi driver said, 'Where do you think you're goin'?' I said, 'I'm going to go to the track.' He said, 'Oh, no, you're not going to get in there.' I said, 'Oh, yes, I am.' Eddie ran there, and of course he had the same problem that he had had a lot of times out of town — that no one would shake hands with him."

Eddie Dugger wasn't the only one who had trouble competing in college athletics. In 1939, Boston College football was in its heyday. The Eagles, led by star running back, Lou Montgomery, won a berth in the Cotton Bowl. But while the team was cheered by thousands of loyal Massachusetts fans in Dallas on New Years Day, Lou Montgomery, an African-American, was back in Boston. Black football players were not welcome in the South.

"Sure I hate not being there," Montgomery said, "but I know there isn't a man on the team that doesn't hate the fact that I can't be there." Boston College lost by three points to Clemson.[24]

Muriel Snowden — who would later found Roxbury's Freedom House with her husband, Otto — also faced racial discrimination in college. When she started earning her degree in sociology from Radcliffe, Muriel was forced to live off the Cambridge campus, apparently because the presence of a Black coed was too disturbing to the sensibilities of Southern girls who came to Radcliffe. After her mother created a fuss, Muriel was allowed to stay in the dormitory her sophomore, junior, and senior years.[25] Noting the parallel to the attempted exclusion of Black freshmen from Harvard dorms in 1922, one wonders whether the Southern students were thought to be less offended by Blacks after a year in a Northern city — or whether, after investing a year's study, the Southerners were less likely to quit school over the issue.

Discrimination in college was perhaps a good preparation for what could be encountered later in many professions. Madeline Kountze Dugger Kelley recalls how difficult it was for her son Edward to find a position in aeronautical engineering after graduating from Tufts:

"His greatest problem was trying to get a job here after he graduated from Tufts. They would not give him a job because he was Black. He was an engineer, ... aeronautical engineer graduate. But they said, 'No, he couldn't be over other people.' He could be a mechanic, but not an engineer. So he took the Civil Service exam, and he passed the exam very high, and he went out to Wright Field, Ohio, where he not only became an ... aeronautical engineer, but he was writing papers and flying all around the country for the Air Force. They've since even named an auditorium for him...."

33

Chapter Four

The '40s

Interlude for World War II

A half million African-Americans served overseas during World War II, dwarfing the sacrifices of Blacks who fought in World War I. The political advances of the '40s — and there were many — were paid for in full on battlefields from Brittany to the Coral Sea.

During WWII, Black Bostonians served as both enlisted personnel and officers in every branch of the Armed Services. There had been significant changes in the military since WWI, but Black soldiers — as evidenced by the following stories of Boston veterans — still had to fight discrimination in their own ranks, as well as the enemy in the field.

Paul Parks, who would later serve as Massachusetts Secretary of Education and Model Cities Administrator in Boston, was born in Indianapolis and drafted into the Army from Purdue University in 1942:

"I wasn't supposed to be drafted out, because I was supposed to get a deferment. But the university recommended that I get drafted immediately..., mainly because I could not stay on campus. No Black person could stay in any dormitory, and I had been leading the fight at that time for dormitory space.

"I was in the segregated Army. A good 'for-instance': ...I went to Richmond one day and I was getting on the bus. And ... I stepped back to let this Black female on in front of me..., and a white soldier behind me said, 'Don't let that Black bitch on in front of you.' And I turned and hit him, and people piled off the bus. There was a first-class riot that occurred in Richmond down in the State House Square.... And I was called in by the Deputy Commander of the post, who happened to be a Black Lieutenant Colonel.... And he told me that I was wrong.... So then at that point he told me that for punishment that he wanted me to go and put on my dress uniform and they would issue me some white gloves and I should open the doors for the white officers and their wives at the white officers club. And I told him, 'Nothing doing.' ... And that's when they sent me under guard — they had two MPs take me to Camp Shanks, New York, and they put me on a boat headed for North Africa."

During the war, Parks almost created a riot at a USO in Paris, where American troops could stay while they were on leave from active duty in Europe:

"There were two USOs in Paris — one for Blacks and one for white soldiers.... And I remember I came out of Germany for a rest leave in Paris, and I wasn't thinking, you know, I was tired. And they made us check our arms as we came into the city and you picked them up when you left. But what they didn't realize was that I was also carrying a revolver, an automatic weapon, that I always carried in the back of my belt.... And I went into this USO at Rainbow Corners, and told them that I was checking in, and they said, 'Well you can't check in here.' And I said, 'Why not?' And they said, 'Because Negro soldiers can't stay in this place. You have to go around the corner.' ... So I said, 'I'm not going.' He said 'Well, I'll call the MPs to put you out.' So I pulled my service revolver, I mean my automatic weapon.... And he disappeared behind the desk. And then there was a big furor and they called the MPs, and this MP Major came with a big bullhorn and asked me if he could come in, and I said, 'Of course.' So he came in and asked what was going on, and I explained to him what had taken place.... 'I came from up in Germany, and I've been in the mud and dirt for all these months and years,' and, I said, 'I've had it. And, if I've got to fight somebody, I might just as well fight the war right here, because this is more relevant to me, you know.' ... So he finally came back and said, 'We have arranged for you to have a hotel room in one of the nicest hotels in Paris.'"

Otto Snowden's father may well have been the Lieutenant Colonel who sent Paul Parks packing to North Africa after Parks started the riot in Richmond, Virginia. After Otto had been drafted, the Army sent him first to Fort Devens, then to Camp Lee, where he says his father was at one time the only Black officer on the post:

"I was drafted. I fought to keep—for getting out of the war, because I resented going into a segregated Army. I tried to beat the draft, but I couldn't do it, so I went.... And the first incident drove me up the side of the wall was a Sergeant saying, 'All you Black boys get over heah, and all you whites get over theah....'

"But I had some influence, so that I would stay there [Fort Devens] only a few days, then I was transferred down to Camp Lee, Virginia, where my father was a high-ranking officer.... And then I made a deal with my father that I wouldn't embarrass him, because he was a Colonel.... And my theory was that now is not the time for fighting [segregation]. Let's win the war, and then we can fight like hell afterwards.... At that time I made up my mind. I wasn't going to do a damn thing in the Army, but stay around here. That's what I did for 42 months. I taught; I wasn't going anywhere. I wasn't going to fight anybody."

It was fortunate for the Army and the war effort that Otto Snowden decided to compromise. He had already shown a talent for organized resistance, even in high school:

"In the late '20s, when I was at the Lewis School [in Roxbury], I organized the first athletic boycott, I think, in the country. There was racism in that school. The principal ... wouldn't allow any Blacks in the orchestra.... But a number of Blacks were going to Lewis School; we controlled the track team. But that man [the principal] was a racist. So I decided one day—before a big track meet—I took the whole team out to lunch. And none of us showed up for the meet, and so the school lost. And I would do things like that. I would take nothing.... "

Royal Bolling Sr. was attending Howard University when the war broke out, and he was called into the Army during the first semester of his senior year, even though he was in the Reserve Officers Training Corps (ROTC):

"And the only thing they would do was guarantee that we'd have an opportunity to go to Officers Candidate School.... That was the first time this had ever been done [drafting people out of college ROTC programs].... So that when I eventually went to Officers Candidate School, we were in a big group with college students from Mississippi,

New Hampshire, from all over the country.... That was an integrated class, when the Army itself was still segregated."

Once commissioned, Bolling became one of the "Buffalo Soldiers" of the racially segregated 92nd Infantry Division, based in Arizona:

"I was very resentful of the fact that this was a segregated thing and nearly all the officers were white — especially the higher-ranking officers. And even, at one time, they had a separate mess [dining facility] for the white officers and the Black officers, until the Black officers raised so much hell that they cut that out.... Just before I joined the 92nd Division, there had been a riot on the post.... And there had been a number of riots on ... other Army posts over the same issues. In the 92nd Division, they finally integrated all their facilities.... Before we went overseas, we had Black company commanders...."

Nonetheless, the only Black majors, lieutenant colonels, or colonels in the segregated 92nd Division were chaplains or people in non-combat roles. The Black company commanders were only ranked as high as captains; in combat, Bolling recalls, this caused problems:

"Well, the weaknesses showed up when we got in combat, because the white officers that were in command really didn't have confidence in the troops that they commanded. And once we got into war situations,... the morale of the officers was terrible. And then the lieutenants and the Black captains, and so forth, they were the ones that really took the leadership roles in active combat."

Bolling was awarded the Purple Heart, the Combat Infantry Badge, four battle stars, and the Silver Star.

Madeline Kountze Dugger Kelley recalls her experience as director of Black service clubs at Fort Devens and later at Camp Miles Standish:

"The service clubs were definitely segregated.... When I went down to Camp Miles Standish, it was even more so. When the soldiers came back, it almost created a riot, because ... they felt, since they had been fighting, we shouldn't have segregated service clubs. But, there was a good side, because we had all the best artists and entertainers ...."

While at Fort Devens, Madeline Dugger also met 2nd Lt. Edward Brooke of Washington, D.C., who would resettle in Boston for a bright political career after the war.

Chapter Five

The '40s

On the Home Front

Ed Cooper, in his mid-'30s when World War II began, stayed home to fight a different battle. In 1942, he stopped managing a First National supermarket store to become Industrial Relations Secretary and then Executive Director of the Urban League in Boston. In some of the nation's defense-related industries, Blacks were moving into higher-paid work, but in Boston the effect of President Roosevelt's Fair Employment Practices program was difficult to gauge — at least early in the decade.

"My job with the Urban League," he recalls, "was in industrial relations, getting jobs for Black people. Between 1942 and 1948, ninety percent of the jobs that the Urban League got in Boston were either domestic jobs or menial jobs. In 1945, the department stores hired their first Black salesperson. In 1946, the New England Telephone Company hired their first [Black] telephone operator. In 1947, the insurance companies hired their first [Black] clerical worker."

Michael Haynes recalls:

"I can see and hear Ed Cooper, the rumors of getting more Blacks on the police force — that's the '40s, not the '50s, with Shag Taylor being the key to get these Black men on the police force — and seeing these new Black police officers after seeing very very few in my lifetime. And then, a lot of it started to happen in the latter part of the '40s, when pressure for Blacks to be probation officers and all these things started stirring."

Picket lines at Dudley

Marcus Mitchell, who would become the first curator of the

Museum of Afro-American History in the late '60s and later Public Relations Director of METCO, arrived in Boston in 1947:

"Another thing that shook me was I came into South Station and I found whites doing all the menial work and the service work. And then, riding by cab to Hotel Lucille through the South End, I saw men of my age standing on each corner and not working — this was work hours! And I told my wife, I said: 'This doesn't look good to me. Not for me and work.'

"Well I did apply at the Navy Yard for a position as a draftsman, and I did have experience. I was interviewed. But I was told that I needed 15 years experience, and I was looking right at a young fellow — couldn't have been, not over 21 — working at a drafting table right in that department. And the other irony was that they were using Bureau of Ships books, many of them holding my illustrations!"

By this time, Boston Blacks were making shrill demands for equal employment opportunities. One of the logical places to begin was the color line in their own community. Mitchell recalls the thriving shopping center around Dudley Station:

"Dudley Street area was a good shopping area, had many stores, and attracted people citywide. But there were no Blacks as sales persons within the stores. There were janitors and the like, but no one working behind the counter."

Michael Haynes comments:

"The only Black person I knew doing anything around Dudley terminal, in my growing up was the Black man who swept Dudley Station,... I think his name was Mr. Nobles.... And the other Black that I remember, a lady ... whose last name was ... Gray, and she was the elevator operator in Timothy Smith's Department Store at Dudley Station. And these were the only Blacks that had status around Dudley Station in my childhood. And the only thing that Blacks did was go into these stores and buy. I can recall Mrs. [Melnea] Cass leading a picket line at Woolworth's Five and Ten on Washington Street.... And we were told not to go into Woolworth's Five and Ten to buy anything; they'd be out there picketing...."

If Mrs. Cass was a general, Marcus Mitchell was a volunteer foot soldier in the battle to see more Blacks working in Dudley-area stores:

"I remember I was on the line. And before that time, they arrested the pickets on the line, and then [the protest leaders] asked that four of us go on that line as a test. And I was the Black chosen to go [laughter] with three whites. The ACLU [American Civil Liberties Union] representative was there, and it was a test case. And I remember a [police] sergeant telling the ACLU representative, who was a minister, that he should be in his pulpit and not bothering with the problems of Blacks.... And he had moved in on me, and asked me why I wasn't satisfied with what was going on in the store, because they did have a janitor there and, you know, a woman working cleaning. I told him what I thought about the Constitution.... So he slammed me against the plate-glass window of Dudley — almost through it."

Ed Cooper recalls the snowball effect of each breakthrough in employment:

"Seeing Blacks on the police force encouraged other Blacks to want to be policemen. Seeing Black firemen encouraged other Blacks to want to be firemen. Seeing Black lawyers and Black teachers encouraged other Blacks to go into teaching.... Because, you see, if you have no role models to look up to, you're chances of getting ahead have been minimized."

Segregation steals into schools

Returning Black veterans were eligible for GI Bill stipends to defray college expenses. Marcus Mitchell, who had been in the Navy, was among the many who came to Boston to take advantage of this opportunity. He also expected his daughter to benefit from the move, but was "shocked" to find segregation in the Boston public schools:

"I came to Boston in the end of summer 1947.... And I was attracted to Boston for educational reasons. One, for myself, I was interested in MIT, because I had been working as a draftsman for the Bureau of Ships in Washington. And I had heard of the wonderful education within Boston, ... higher education as well as public school education. We ... had one daughter, and we didn't like the segregated system in Washington, D.C., so we wanted to bring her here. She was finishing kindergarten, and she would then be entering first grade.... It [the school system in Boston] was given high points by the Ebony publication, and we believed what we read...."

Segregation in Boston schools was something relatively new. It had something to do with the increasing numbers and distribution of Blacks in the population, because there had been no segregation in earlier decades, Elma Lewis recalls:

"There were very few — maybe there were 20,000 Black people in Boston when I was a child [in the '20s and '30s]. Therefore I never went to a Black school. There were not enough children to make one. Schools were always mixed population."

Here's how John O'Bryant, who in 1978 would become the first Black person in this century to win a seat on the Boston School Committee, describes the school situation at the end of the '40s:

"Well, I was in college between 1948 and 1952.... And one of the reasons why I was involved was because the NAACP was actively trying to get the School Department to recognize the inherent inequity in segregation. It was at that time when we had probably about eight to ten schools that were segregated because of neighborhood patterns, and Boston had the neighborhood school concept at the time. People went to the school closest to their home. And Ruth Batson and others who were active with the NAACP Education Committee were trying to point out to the school administrators and policymakers that the Black kids were not getting a fair shake, primarily because the resources were not evenly distributed. A number of permanent teachers would transfer out of the predominantly Black schools and go to the white schools, which would leave the predominantly Black schools with a lot of temporary and inexperienced teachers.... Some of these youngsters would have as many as 12 or 13 teachers in one year."

O'Bryant says about 95 percent of the teachers in the schools were white at this time:

"And there were no Black principals and no Black guidance counselors. Not one. Not one.... I was the first Black guidance counselor appointed in this whole school system.... I was officially appointed in 1966, when I went to English High School. But I was serving in an acting capacity at Technical High School in the late '50s and early '60s."

❖ ❖ ❖

Even for middle-class African-Americans, alternatives to the pub-

lic schools were difficult to find in the '40s. David Nelson, who would run for Congress in the '70s and serve as both a state and federal Judge, could not go to a parochial school — despite belonging to the small but growing group of Black Catholics in Boston. He recalls:

"I couldn't go to parochial school because I was Black, although I heard every Sunday that it was a sin for parents not to send their kids to parochial schools. I guess it wasn't a sin for Black families."[26]

When St. Richard's, a mission for Blacks and Indians, was built in Roxbury, Nelson recalls the pastor at St. Joseph's telling Blacks in his congregation, "You people are not to come here any more; you're to go to your church over there."[27] Nelson, whose Jamaica-born father was a union organizer for the Amalgamated Clothing Workers of America, also could not serve as an altar boy at St. Joseph's because he was Black.

In the mid-'40s, Mel King was in high school, wondering where and how he would go to college:

"The guidance counselor at my high school — and I use the term 'guidance counselor' loosely ... never encouraged us to attend college and never made it known to me that there was a college up the street, Boston Teachers College, that I could have attended for, at that point, less than $50...."

King, who would represent the South End in the state legislature from 1973 to 1982, also recalls being misinformed by officials at nearby Northeastern University:

"When I finished Technical High School and expressed an interest in going there [Northeastern University], I was told that because I hadn't a [foreign] language I wouldn't be able to attend. And it turns out that several of the people who attended Technical High School with me were able to attend [Northeastern] because they were told that they could take four regular courses and one remedial [foreign language] course to get their language requirement up. So they were in; I never got in. And perhaps I would have attended there, because it was in the neighborhood."

King ended up going to all-Black Claflin College in South Carolina on an athletic scholarship. Michael Haynes says he wondered at the time why King and other Blacks were not offered scholarships at northern colleges closer to home:

"Toward the latter part of the '40s, ... Blacks went away to colleges, not being able to get scholarships in colleges up north. And I can remember when Mel King left Boston to go to college in Claflin in South Carolina, and I did a little story on it for the *Boston Chronicle*: Why did he have to go all the way to South Carolina, as good an athlete as he was?"

If Boston schools had few Black teachers, suburban schools had far fewer. Madeline Kountze Dugger Kelley recalls her daughter, Barbara, trying to do her practice teaching in Medford, where she had been an outstanding student before going to college:

"Barbara, when she got ready to do her practice teaching, was told that she could not teach in Medford because she was Black. They were not going to have a Black teacher over white children. That was about 1942, the early '40s. And so I came home from Fort Devens, where I was at the time, and went to the School Committee. They said they couldn't do much about it. I went to the [state] Department of Education downtown. They said they couldn't do much about it, about *their* superintendent, but he was going to have to let her teach.

"So, Barbara was finally let go up to Hervey School up here; they let her walk up and down the hall. They wouldn't give her a class. I went up there. I said, 'What are you walking up and down the hall for?' She said, 'They won't give me a class, and they said they'll give me bad marks because of the Superintendent.' And she never got a poor mark in her life — all A's! So I told them they had to do something about it. So, finally, the Department of Education told them they had to let her teach. So she did her practice teaching. By that time I was out at Camp Miles Standish, and Dr. Charlotte Hawkins Brown [nationally prominent educator who founded Palmer Memorial Institute] called me and said, 'Can't we have your daughter down here; she would be a great example.' ... And so I finally let Barbara go to the Charlotte Hawkins Brown School in North Carolina, where she worked and lived."

It would take Medford another decade — until 1952 — to appoint its first Black school teacher. But in 1963, the city would take a much bigger step, electing another of Madeline Kountze Dugger Kelley's daughters, Madeline D. Andrews, to the Medford School Committee — and apparently establishing her as the first Black woman elected to public office in Massachusetts.

The Jeffersons' dream house

The Veterans Administration offered soldiers returning from the war attractive housing subsidies, as well as college stipends. Matthew Jefferson would become the first elected Black official in Newton and spend 20 years on the Newton Board of Aldermen, six of those years as Board President. He recalls how difficult it could be in the '40s for Blacks to find decent housing in this Boston suburb — even if they qualified for veterans' benefits:

"I remember, as a young person coming out of the military, I had sufficient monies for down payments in a house. And my desire was to buy a single-family house in Newton. I liked Newton, because my wife came from Newton.

"And I came out of the service, and we went looking for a house, and we were told by realtors in no uncertain terms that they would not sell us a home if it was not in a — at that time they called it a 'colored neighborhood.' And we weren't necessarily looking for housing outside of the so-called colored neighborhood. But what we were looking for was substantial good housing. And one of the things that happened in the Village [the area in Newton where most Blacks lived], and in the particular so-called colored neighborhood at that time, is that the housing was ... all occupied. I mean ... there was just no room for expansion. There was no room for building anything else! And if you wanted a larger house, and if you couldn't get a pick out of that particular area where the houses were all occupied, then your choices were limited.... So we looked and we looked — and to no avail.... But eventually, we returned to that particular neighborhood, where we found a house — dilapidated as it was — and for the next 25 years we worked on it, and we made it a home....

"But that was the plight that we were working against back in 1946. And there were no rules, or no laws, at that time prohibiting discrimination in housing — when a realtor could tell you that they would not sell you a house. They would not show you a house, because they felt that, quote, 'The property value would decrease' and that kind of thing."

Having found their house, the Jeffersons were not content to drop the issue of fair housing. Jefferson's wife, Lillie, who had moved with her family to Newton from North Carolina in 1929, recalls Blacks and whites organizing around the housing issue in the late '40s:

"Out of the Myrtle Baptist Church came a lot of the things that have made a difference in Newton. For instance, when we began fair housing issues in Newton, the beginnings of that were people meeting together, Black and white people, meeting together in Myrtle Baptist Church, and determining that they were going to form a Newton Fair Housing Committee. And that committee [in about 1948] was the beginning of open housing [in Newton]....

"And we got together, and we did the petitions, we lobbied ... and we went up and down the streets and got signatures of people saying they were willing to deal with open housing."

Housing progress came slowly, Matthew Jefferson recalls:

"Well, let's put it this way.... It took at least ten years to where you began to see the 'light at the end of the tunnel.' Where you could walk up, and you didn't have to have a straw [a white person] to buy a house for you, or to intercede for you."

Housing discrimination was, of course, not hard to find in Boston in the '40s. In 1943, Ebenezer Baptist Church was looking for a "church school" building. They tried to buy a house at 80 Worcester Street, but the sales agent didn't want Black people on that part of the street. So Rev. William S. Ravenell made a special trip to New York, where he persuaded the owner to sell the building.[28]

The real estate business

Thinking that a lot of Black veterans would be able to afford to buy homes after the war, Royal Bolling Sr. decided to go to work in a real estate office owned by Edward J. Rosten, one of the city's first Black trolley-car drivers. Selling the house, Bolling discovered, was only the first step:

"When I really became active in the real estate business, it was difficult to sell a house. But then, when you finally got a customer who said, 'Okay, I'll buy that house,' and you go out and try to get the financing for them, and bank after bank turns the customer down, you begin to think, 'There's something wrong here.' And then I learned that nearly every bank in Boston — it was unusual for them to have any mortgages that were given to Blacks....

"And then, if we were able to sell the house, get the financing in place, then we found out that the insurance companies were not willing to insure the properties. They had redlined certain areas, and were refusing to give insurance in those areas."

All the problems seemed to point Bolling toward the political arena:

"I said, if these conditions are going to exist, then I'm certainly not going to be in business very long. So I inquired around as to how you could combat this discrimination. And I came to the conclusion that it was in the field of politics that it could be approached."

Politics — into the mainstream

Now packed into the South End and Roxbury, Blacks in Boston in the '40s were beginning to establish themselves as a political force, particularly in Ward 9 in the South End. Throughout the decade, Blacks poured into Boston in record numbers. The Black population of the city increased 70 percent during the decade — from 23,679 in 1940 to 40,157 in 1950, or from 3.1 percent to 5 percent of the total population of the city.[29]

As a consequence, Blacks were no longer satisfied to be a mere sidelight to political campaigns. Otto Snowden recalls the embarrassment this caused Christian Herter, a white Republican who served in the Massachusetts House from '43 to '53 and as Governor from '53 to '57:

"Chris Herter ... I think he was running for the House. Blacks were really part of his campaign. But each time he ran, he'd have a Black dinner for them at one of the hotels. And I think I organized — somebody got up, one of the oldtimers, got up and said we didn't appreciate the segregated support, that we wanted to be part of his major campaign. And it really shook poor Chris Herter, because he was a very good guy. He just thought this was the way to do it — have all the Blacks together...."

A Black pioneer

Those like Royal Bolling Sr. who were eyeing electoral politics in the post-war period were both inspired and embittered by the experience of Lawrence Banks. Michael Haynes has a dim recollection of this political pioneer:

"Haskins Street in the '40s: The apartment house that was once Jewish and Black is now all Black, and there's a man living in there that's a lawyer. His sign is in his window, too.... Lawrence, I think it was 'Lawrence H. Banks', if memory serves me good, 'Lawrence H. Banks, Attorney at Law.' ... Now he seemed to be a rather passive man, as I recollect him. He didn't seem to be very very aggressive, he didn't seem like a football quarterback at all. Lawrence was very very passive and very very gentle."

And amazingly tenacious! Lawrence Banks was not the type of politician that simply followed the crowd. In a time and place that saw many Blacks turning Democrat, particularly in Ward 9, Banks made a career of repeatedly running for office as a Republican.

For instance, in 1942 Banks was defeated in a campaign for the State House by Dennis Glynn, a white Democrat. That year enrolled Democrats in Ward 9 outnumbered enrolled Republicans by more than 3 to 1 (6,549 to 1,815). That didn't deter Banks. In 1944, Glynn defeated him again. In 1945, Banks lost a close City Council election to Daniel Sullivan, who would hold the Ward 9 (South End) seat until 1951.[30]

In 1946, Banks finally broke through to electoral victory. He defeated his old nemesis, Dennis Glynn, 4,753 to 3,900 to become the first African-American from Boston to serve in the Massachusetts legislature in the 20th century — and the state's first Black State Representative since 1902, when William H. Lewis represented Cambridge.

John Bynoe remembers a lot of World War II veterans working on the Banks campaign:

"We came back as veterans, and we organized to get Larry Banks elected Representative.... We went out and watched the streets, carried banners, got people uplifted, thinking about it."

When Dennis Glynn recaptured the Ward 9 House seat in 1948 (6,037 to 5,151), some thought they saw a white backlash in the size of the vote — and in a new set of election laws passed by the City Council that year. "Plan A," as the charter reform was called, would not take effect until 1951, when the old system of electing a councilor from each of the city's 22 wards would be scrapped in favor of electing only nine at-large city councilors.

City charter reform

Plan A would force each council candidate to campaign citywide — and that meant a Black candidate could not be elected without winning in white neighborhoods. Some Black leaders opposed the plan, convinced it was intended to prevent the election of Black city councilors; others supported it as a way to clean up city government. Getting anything through a group of 22 councilors, each representing a different section of the city, must have been challenging, to say the least.

John Bynoe, who supported the change, thought of it as a "strong-mayor charter":

"Well, we [supporters of John Hynes, who was elected Mayor in 1949] were part of the change — 1949. We voted for a new form of government ... [that] gave much more administrative responsibilities to the mayor.... The advantage was to get rid of them thieves [in city government].... Everybody was on the take."

Although the Black wards (9 and 12) were certainly not the only ones that were weakened politically by the change in election laws, Blacks in general perceived the city charter change as at least partially racist. Michael Haynes recalls the reaction:

"I was in school at the time. I just remember reverberations on it — that they were changing the form of government to keep Blacks from getting office. They were gerrymandering; they were changing lines and everything else. Everything was being done to keep Blacks out of office."

Mel King sees a direct link between the charter reform of 1948 and the massive, sometimes destructive urban renewal that began in Boston a year after the first at-large Council was seated in 1952:

"I think that, although they were able to capitalize on the issue of race, that ... they didn't have to talk about it for people who were not interested in seeing Black people in political positions. They had this as a vehicle, however. The reason for the vehicle has to do with what you're looking at downtown now — the intent to be able to develop, in brick and mortar terms, the city. They knew they couldn't do it [with] the 22-member council — where each of the councilors is going to look out for their own interests. And I think one of the ways you can see how that works ... is that no part of the city where a councilor lived got an urban renewal program.... And so the interesting thing is that those councilors from South Boston, and West Roxbury, and East Boston were the ones who voted for urban renewal in the South End, Jamaica Plain, and other parts of the city, Roxbury.... So that's what that nine-person council accomplished.... You can buy off those folks better at-large than you could by district."

Urban renewal, as we shall see in the next chapter, becomes one the hottest political issues of the '50s.

A stolen election

The Black community reacted even more bitterly a year later, in 1949. Again, Lawrence Banks challenged Sullivan for the Ward 9 Council seat. When the official count left Banks trailing by six votes, he accused the Democrats of tampering with the ballots. Banks took his case to court, where a Massachusetts judge declared him winner of the Council race. There was jubilation among Banks supporters, until the Democrats on the City Council voted to leave Sullivan in office, pending his appeal to the state Supreme Court. To the City Councilors, Banks had three shortcomings: He was an outsider, a Black, and a Republican!

By the time the upper court had rejected Sullivan's appeal, only three months remained for Banks to enjoy his seat on the Council, although he received full retroactive pay for the 21 months he had missed. In the meantime, the ever-active Banks had lost another run for state representative.

Michael Haynes recalls the reaction in the Black community to the legal and political maneuvering that kept Banks off the Council for 21 months:

"Yes, there was a lot of tension, a lot of bitterness in the community over the Lawrence Banks issue. It was surely prevalent on my street, because he lived on Haskins Street. It was very prevalent there."

James Jennings, a Black political scientist, has said of the Banks victory that it was the "culmination of the Black community before World War II, getting what it had been groping for in the past 20 to 30 years."[31]

Banks could never have won a Council seat without solid support in the Black community — Republican and Democrat. Ed Cooper credits Shag Taylor with providing the Democratic support — and for working regularly with Black Republicans for the good of the community:

"Shag Taylor? He was supportive of Lawrence Banks, notwithstanding the fact that Banks was a Republican. Because the important thing to remember is that, although Shag was a Democrat and Wilfred Scott was a Republican, they were good friends. Shag knew that he had his job to do as a Democrat, and Scott knew he had his job to do as a Republican. And I think, if either one of them hadn't supported the other, we wouldn't have gotten along as well as we did."

Another Democrat who helped Banks was attorney Henry Quarles Sr.:

"Lawrence lived with me up in Roxbury for a while, and he had a place down on Corn Hill [a fashionable downtown street that no longer exists] as a multigrapher.... If a friend was running, you didn't care if he was a Republican or a Democrat.... When he went back to Ward 9 [in the South End], ... I used to go down and write his speeches out for him."

Banks would never have another chance for a seat on the Council; the new election system made further victories in his day virtually impossible. Thomas Atkins would win an at-large seat in 1967 — but by that time, there would be twice as many Blacks in Boston as there were in '49.

Did it have to be that way? Or was the resistance to Banks among white voters and politicians something peculiar to race relations in Boston?

The example of Herbert Jackson

In 1945, the same year Banks was losing a City Council bid in Boston, Herbert Jackson ran for a City Council seat in Malden, just a few miles north. Jackson, whose father was a successful tailor in Malden, ran for office from heavily Jewish Ward 7 and won. By 1947, he was no longer living in Ward 7, but in the much larger and heavily Protestant Ward 5. No problem. Jackson was elected from Ward 5. In 1950, Jackson expanded his base, running a successful campaign to represent Malden at the State House. After two terms on Beacon Hill, Jackson was denied a third term by a mere 245 votes in 1954. But he soon sought and repeatedly won election as an at-large City Councilor, competing for the votes of the entire Malden electorate. Jackson was elected Council President in '49, '65, '71, and '75. When he retired from the City Council in 1975, he had spent some 30 years in public office.

When Malden built a new City Hall after Herbert Jackson's death in 1978, the new Council Chambers were named in his honor.

That Jackson was an extraordinary man there is little doubt. An accomplished actor, he is described as handsome, dynamic, exciting —

much more so than Lawrence Banks. Nonetheless, one can wonder what the tenor of race relations in Boston would be today if Banks had been welcomed onto Boston's City Council the way Jackson apparently was accepted in Malden. What if Banks had become a voice for those who suddenly found their children attending inferior, segregated schools? We don't know, and we will never know. But the example of Herbert Jackson and the voters of Malden lends credibility to speculation that things might have been significantly different.

Freedom House

Lawrence Banks was not, of course, all that was going on in the Black politics of Boston in the late '40s. When Muriel and Otto Snowden founded Freedom House in 1948, few could have foreseen the significant role it would play in the coming decades. At the time, Otto recalls, the primary intent was to keep Roxbury integrated:

"We had reached the tipping point in Roxbury then. It was predominantly white. Let's say it [was] maybe 60 percent white, 40 percent Black. And we were trying to keep it from — we didn't want the white people to move. But, unfortunately, it was right after the war, and it was a seller's market, and you could get a good price for your house.... The lower part of Roxbury was Irish, but a small percentage of Irish. And the middle — from the lower up to the middle — was Black. The upper part was Jewish....

"Basically, we wanted to keep the community from deteriorating. We didn't want it all-Black. We wanted it integrated. If it had to be all-Black, we wanted it to be the best Black community in Boston. We were certain about the schools. We wanted parent participation in those schools. We wanted the streets clean, that type of thing."

The sixteen co-founders of Freedom House included Wilfred Scott, Melnea Cass, and Lucy Mitchell. For years, Otto would work full-time without pay. To provide income for the family, Muriel headed the Civic Unity Committee in Cambridge, helping out evenings and weekends at Freedom House.

Redbaiting

America's post-war struggle with the Soviet Union left leaders of the American left — and some who were not leftists —vulnerable to charges of being Communists. Otto Snowden, a Republican, was among the Black leaders who were forced to defend themselves:

"They called me a Communist, that the organization [Higginson Home and School Association, which Otto Snowden was heading] was taken over by Communist Otto Snowden. So I went to the newspapers and said, 'That's a lie.' So the *Boston Herald,* the *Traveler* then, did an editorial. 'The issue was not the Snowdens,... but what they wanted.' Because nobody reads editorials, I had about 10,000 editorials reprinted and gave it to the community. They were trying to make us Communists!"

Michael Haynes recalls the vicious redbaiting of the late '40s:

"It seems like everyone that rose up to speak out against racial discrimination during my childhood, someone would be trying to label them pink or red. And that's clear in my head....

"In the late '40s, I started writing a column for the Boston Chronicle. And that brought me into a relationship with ... a guy by the name of Bill Harrison, who was a Black graduate of Harvard.... And I was scared of this guy — this guy was a [reputed] 'Communist'! And I got to where I found him to be a wonderful guy. He encouraged me in church ... The man never did anything but encourage the best of the Americanism that was in me. And that forever stayed in my mind."

In was through Harrison that Marcus Mitchell met James Michael Curley. His recollection of a connection between Mayor Curley and Harrison throws a different light on Mayor Curley, the Curley of the '40s:

"Well, Curley had a way with the poor by helping one family on a street, and it misled people into thinking he was a great knight, ... but it was a misguided thing; it misled the Blacks. I think Bill Harrison served as a ghost writer for Curley.... And I know that he [Harrison] had helped many of us, not only Curley, but others, with speeches and the like. And so, it was through him that I was able to see Curley."

Mitchell also recalls Curley's reaction to an appearance of W.E.B. DuBois, then editor of *The Crisis* magazine for the NAACP:

"The left brought Dr. DuBois into town to speak at Ruggles Hall. And Curley ... did his redbaiting, and set up a meeting at Faneuil Hall. And the next day, in the paper, he's cursing the people of Boston because there were only, I think, about 45 turned up at Faneuil Hall — it was an All-American day flag wave. And Ruggles Hall was jammed with people."

What a picture of Curley — a redbaiting anti-Communist who secretly had Bill Harrison writing his populist rhetoric.

Paul Robeson

Paul Robeson — who was an All-America football player at Rutgers University, a first-rate singer, and the foremost Black actor of his time — was another persecuted leftist who inspired many Blacks in the '40s, including Mel King, who says of Robeson: "Perhaps more than anyone else except my own father, Robeson was an early influence that got me involved and ready for the work to come."[32]

Sarah-Ann Shaw — who helped organize Stop Day, the Boston Action Group boycotts, and the public school stayouts of the '60s and later become a television news reporter — recalls a Robeson performance in Boston that was cut short by police, ostensibly because the hall he appeared in was overcrowded:

"I remember my father taking me to hear Paul Robeson at the old Masonic Temple, which was on Tremont Street. And I remember the police coming in and stopping Robeson's performance. They claimed, according to my father, that the hall was too crowded. But my father and others felt that it was his political views.... It was a rally — a minister spoke and they had some choir singing — and Robeson sang and was supposed to speak, but he didn't get to speak, ... or he didn't get to finish his speech, because the police came in and made everyone leave. And I remember being so frightened and not understanding."

Marcus Mitchell also recalls Robeson:

"Paul Robeson came under attack. And we were the youth of the day, and we invited Robeson — to show our stand — to visit the South End. And we put him up for three days and traveled around the city with him. A lot of the Black leadership were afraid to even be seen with Robeson around that time [because of charges that he was a Communist]. But then we were shocked to find out that Robeson was admired by many in Boston. And he had a meeting at the Masonic Hall on Tremont Street near St. Cyprians, and there was a united front, or turnout of Blacks of all political persuasions there. Robeson didn't talk politics, but more about music, about world culture.... So what I'm saying is that that label didn't affect the community — the label, the

Communist label, or the left-wing label. We would move in a group, or body, to come together to support each other."

Michael Haynes recalls another victim of anti-Communist innuendo, Father Kenneth DePauline Hughes, rector of St. Bartholomews Episcopal Church in Cambridge and President of the Boston NAACP in 1946-47:

"As a kid, I can remember him taking positions, either as the President of the NAACP or as the spokesman for the NAACP, I'm not sure. But I do remember him speaking out against discrimination and all these things that were taking place against Black people. Here again, I also remember hearing people saying that he was Communist."

Robert Coard, who would become Director of Action for Boston Community Development (ABCD), also recalls Rev. Hughes:

"He was such a great activist that I think he got censured by his Bishop for knowing Paul Robeson too well, who was a bugaboo in those days."

Of course, after much soul-searching, some thoughtful Blacks — Bill Harrison and Amanda Houston's mother, for instance — did see their struggle as a class struggle, especially during the Depression days of the '30s, when class lines were so clearly drawn. But these Blacks were hardly the destructive force they were made out to be. Amanda Houston recalls her mother's anti-strike-breaking activities in the '30s:

"What she used to do is that she used to ... go into plants that used to import Blacks to break strikes and bring the Blacks back out again, by explaining that their self-interest was best served by working with the striking whites, rather than trying to work for less as Black people.

"There was a laundry in Watertown that the Irish women basically went on strike because of poor working conditions and low wages. And this particular company sent through buses down Tremont Street, down Columbus Avenue in the '30s to pick up Black women to bring them out there. And my mother used to hop on that bus and ... go in with the women and talk with them and bring them out. And they did [come out] in the long run. They were unable to get Black women to continue to come in, and those women did win their strike. The problem was that the white working women's union did not keep their promises to use Black women.... They did bring more Black women in, but they gave them the hardest jobs, such as ironing, which was considered a job for Black women to do...."

By the '40s, many of the Blacks who had leftist leanings were disillusioned. Amanda Houston recalls her mother's feelings:

"She became very disillusioned with the party.... I know that she became more interested in those who were followers of Trotsky.... But the thing that I think thoroughly disillusioned her — she began to believe that there was racism within the Communist Party — subtle racism that they themselves wouldn't address. And that within that racism was the attitude that Blacks should be in the vanguard of the battle ... [but] should not be the planners, thinkers, and intellectuals of the Party...."

Amanda Houston's mother may have been among those who urged Ruth Batson and other Blacks not to move into the segregated Orchard Park housing project, which opened up in the '40s. This is how Batson recalls her decision:

"... When we were going to move into the project, we were approached by groups people said were Communists, saying that they [the buildings at Orchard Park] were going to be segregated, which they were ... and that to move in there would be to bow to this segregated ruling. And I was so desperate for housing, you know, that I said to my husband, ... 'We're going to move into this project; I don't care.' It was segregated anyhow."

Four buildings in the Orchard Park project in Roxbury were set aside for Black families, continuing the segregation policies of the Housing Authority that began in the '30s. Michael Haynes comments on Batson and the project:

"It almost seemed proper that somebody had to emerge out of that project, speaking for people and speaking for tenants, and speaking about the school situation. And Ruth certainly was a pioneer, a young pioneer...."

To understand how much of a pioneer Ruth Batson would be, we must turn to the decade of the '50s.

Chapter Six

The '50s

Gathering Steam

No great historical event overshadows the 1950s the way World War I unleashes the passions of the '20s, the Great Depression frames the '30s, or World War II dominates the '40s. The era of the '50s in Boston is like a vast pressure cooker from which the civil rights movement of the '60s eventually explodes.

The mythical American "melting pot" was in dire need of a vigorous stir in the '50s, but the reactionary anti-Communism of the post-war period seemed hell-bent on breaking anything that seemed likely to create serious waves. In Boston, the intransigence of the white majority that rejected Lawrence Banks and Black representation on the Boston City Council at the end of the '40s was, unfortunately, the spirit of the '50s.

It can be argued that for Boston in the '50s, the epoch-making event should have been the 1954 U.S. Supreme Court decision to drop the "separate but equal" doctrine that had temporarily given constitutional protection to legally segregated schools in the South and to de facto segregation of schools elsewhere. But the ruling fell into a conservative political atmosphere that delayed action on its broad implications.

There was, of course, great rejoicing in the Black community when the high court decision was handed down in 1954.

Ruth Batson was among many Boston Blacks and whites who joined the Parents Federation in the late '40s and early '50s to help improve the Boston public schools. She remembers getting news of the Supreme Court decision from a white friend in this group:

"She said, 'Oh, Ruth, what a happy day — the Supreme Court decision!' And I remember at the time, I didn't even — hadn't heard about the decision. And she told me. And I thought, 'Oh my goodness...!' And we were just delighted. We thought that that was the basis upon which everything could be changed. We really did think it was a big change."

The "big change" Batson and her friend anticipated had to await the dramatic developments of the '60s — and for those events to be realized in Boston, people like Ruth Batson had to push hard throughout the '50s.

For a lesson in holding on and never giving up, Batson could reflect on the career of Lawrence Banks, who continued to mount unsuccessful campaigns for public office. He lost Ward 9 campaigns for the State House in '50, '52, '54, '55, '56, '58, and '60.[33] Batson recalls Banks running for a City Council seat when she campaigned for the School Committee in 1951:

"The only [other] Blacks that I knew who were running [for office] at that point was a man named Lawrence Banks.... Poor Lawrence Banks.... To me, he always appeared to be a very tragic figure,... a very brave man.... It was just the saddest thing."

Batson says she ran for the School Committee, knowing she could not win, as a way of publicizing problems in the public schools:

"You know, I sat around and I thought about it, I talked about it with my girlfriend, and I said to her, 'You know, somebody has to run for the Boston School Committee ... [to] bring out all these things — poor dummy!' And she said, 'That's right, and we'll help you,' and so forth. And we were really completely naive...."

Ruth Batson's 1951 campaign foreshadowed the Black community's assault on the School Committee in the 1960s, which culminated in the election of John O'Bryant in 1977. It is significant that Batson and those who followed in her footsteps — Mel King and O'Bryant — were not in any way connected to the traditional Democratic Party leadership. Batson says of Shag Taylor:

"He used to call me 'Miss Boston,' because he said I was so arrogant and thought I knew everything. And which — he was right, you know. But I just wouldn't have thought of it [asking for Taylor's support]. He wouldn't have given it anyway. He was too practical. He was an absolute politician."

When Batson asked a leader of the New Boston Committee, a prominent reform group of the period, why she was not on the committee's slate of candidates, he mentioned "this Communist business." What he referred to was the fact that the Parents Federation had been discredited by the presence of known Communists in its ranks, Batson recalls:

"This woman, who was very active in the Parents Federation, her husband was the noted Communist Otis Hood.... The fact that she was a Communist didn't mean anything to me, you know, but the organization became tainted with this Communist thing, because it was the time of McCarthyism and so forth. And people then started the rumors that I was a Communist. That sort of thing didn't faze me; I just didn't give a damn.... But it did give me a lot of grief, because people were scared to death...."

Needless to say, Batson was not elected to the School Committee, although she did surprise the "experts" by picking up some 16,000 votes, a reflection of growing concern about Boston schools.

After the Parents Federation folded, Ruth Batson went to Boston NAACP President Lionel Lindsay to see what his organization might do to help the public schools:

"... And he said to me, 'Well, Mrs. Batson, I'm sorry, but we don't have any committee that would handle that. We have an Education Committee, but they deal with scholarships and counseling for college....' So I came home, thinking, 'What a dumb organization!' ... I hadn't been home a day, when Lionel called me, and he had talked to some people, and they thought they ought to have a subcommittee called the Public School Committee, and would I like to run it? Well, that's the story of my life, ... because from then on, all I ever did was work on education issues."

In the early '60s, the NAACP would make a significant change: Ruth Batson's committee, which actually began as a subcommittee, would become *the* NAACP Education Committee, to which the old Education Committee would be appended as a subcommittee. The Batson committee would then become the battering ram of the Black community in its battle against segregated schooling and the low quality of education in the Black neighborhood schools.

Storming the State House

Virtually locked out of the City Council by the charter reform of 1948 (which took effect in '51), Black Democrats, following the lead of Shag Taylor, turned their attention to the State House, where they finally tasted victory in 1956 with the election from Ward 9 of Lincoln Pope.

Ruth Batson says of Pope:

"Actually, I met Lincoln through my husband, because they used to wait table together. They had one of these side jobs ... with a caterer.... And he [Pope] was just, you know, everybody loved him. You know, he had a joke all the time. He never seemed to be very serious. Oh, he was lovely looking and very debonair — and had a wonderful speaking voice."

It may seem odd today, but it was not unusual then for Lincoln Pope — a graduate of Boston University — to be waiting tables shortly before his election to the Massachusetts General Court. Ed Cooper, who refers to Lincoln Pope as a "protege of Shag Taylor," explains:

"You see, ... like many other — even educated — Blacks, [Pope] waited tables for parties. And I can name you half a dozen lawyers today in Boston who were Lincoln Pope's peers who came out of law school and couldn't get into business, so they waited tables."

John Bynoe says of the Pope campaign:

"I was working for the government.... Myself, Milton Hardwick, and Doris Bunte [who would later serve in the state legislature and become Director of the Boston Housing Authority] were Lincoln Pope's key people. Shag and Bal [Shag Taylor and his brother, Balcom] were backing him, okay? They were putting the money up, whatever money we spent in those days...."

Lincoln Pope, who was the first Black Democrat to represent Boston on Beacon Hill, was a brother-in-law of Malden's Herbert Jackson and grandson of James W. Pope, who served on the Boston Council in the late-19th century.

The Pope election was both a triumph and a "last hurrah" for Shag Taylor. Two years later, shortly after a large testimonial dinner in his honor, Silas (Shag) Taylor was killed in an automobile accident, John Bynoe recalls:

"I was one of the guys that ran the testimony for him in '58. We just gave a testimonial, then shortly after that he got killed."

John Bynoe says Balcom Taylor tried for a few years to pick up the mantle of leadership that slipped from Shag's shoulders, but the Taylor brothers' drugstore on Tremont Street was no longer the center of Democratic politics in Roxbury.

Perhaps Shag's work was done. He had lived to see the doors to the State House begin to swing open for Boston's Black community — and they would not be slammed shut again, as the doors to the City Council were in the '40s. When "Linc" Pope left office in the early '60s to become Legislative Assistant to the Sergeant at Arms of the House of Representatives, he left behind several elected Black Representatives from Boston — Royal Bolling Sr., Rev. Michael Haynes, and Franklin W. Holgate.

While Pope was establishing himself in the South End and Ward 9, other Black politicians were mounting campaigns for the State House from Ward 12 in Roxbury. Democrat Oswald D. Jordan and Republicans Alfred S. Brothers and Harry J. Elam ran in 1956. In those days, two representatives were elected from Ward 12. The two Black Republicans, Brothers and Elam, won in the preliminary election, but were defeated by the same two white candidates who defeated Jordan in the Democratic primary.

In 1958, Jordan and Brothers ran again in their respective parties. This time Jordan not only won in the Democratic primary, he also received the most votes of any candidate in the final election. Brothers won in the primary, but ran third in the final election, behind white candidate George Green, who took the second House seat from Ward 12. Brothers would be elected in 1960 and again in '62.

Royal Bolling Sr. was edged out in the 1958 Democratic primary for state representative in Ward 12 by Oswald Jordan and George Green. Bolling would defeat Green in 1960 to begin his long and colorful State House career — first in the House and later in the Senate.

Ed Brooke

Another Black candidate of the early '50s was Edward Brooke, who had received LL.B. and LL.M. degrees from Boston University's law school in '48 and '49.

Brooke ran unsuccessful Ward 12 campaigns for the State House in 1950 and again in 1952, gaining experience that would eventually make him one of the most successful Black politicians in the country.

Brooke made a significant decision during the first of those campaigns. At the time, he considered himself a Democrat, but in those days it was legally possible to cross-file — to run in both the Democratic and Republican primaries. Brooke lost as a Democrat in the primary, but won as a Republican. The question was: Should he accept the nomination and run as a Republican in the final election, which would mean changing his registration from Democrat to Republican? The fact that he had many influential Black Republican friends — such as Clarence Elam, who served as Secretary to the Governor's Council, made the change an easy one. Although Brooke lost the election, becoming a Republican would prove to be a significant milestone in his career.

Brooke's decision had little or no impact on his popularity among Democrats, many of whom helped elect him Massachusetts Attorney General and then United States Senator in the '60s. For instance, Victor Bynoe says of Brooke:

"As a Democrat, I thought he was smart. I said, 'Look, man, you did the right thing.' ... You don't run just to run; you run to be successful."

Soon after Brooke switched parties, the law was changed to prevent candidates from running in more than one party primary, but filing as an Independent or a Republican to avoid running in crowded Democratic primaries in Boston is still a popular tactic.

Black population growth
After his 1952 campaign, Brooke retired from politics until he ran unsuccessfully for secretary of state in 1960. He had good reason to feel time was on his side. Blacks were still streaming into Boston in the '50s, if not quite as fast as they had in the '40s. The Black population of the city increased 57 percent in the '50s — down from 70 percent in the '40s. The 1950 Black population of about 40,000 had grown to about 63,000 in 1960.[34]

Marcus Mitchell describes the advantages Southern Blacks — even from a city like Washington, D.C. — found in Boston in the late '40s and early '50s:

"In Washington, D.C., you could not buy in the major stores ... in town. Yet there's a large Black population there.... Black Bostonians ... could trade in the stores. But they did not hold the major positions, as I said, as sales persons. That came later. The FEPC had just been placed on the books at that time. And Elwood McKinney was head of the FEPC

— that's Fair Employment Practices Commission, [which] had just been passed in Massachusetts. So they [Bostonians] had some advantages over Washington."

The Fair Employment Practices Commission

In his FEPC post, attorney Elwood McKinney, who had served as Secretary to the Governor's Council and would later become a Judge in Roxbury District Court, could be extremely helpful to Blacks who experienced discrimination in finding jobs. For instance, in the early '50s, Amanda Houston was working at Raytheon, where she heard there were some openings for machinists at high pay:

"I suggested to my husband that he apply. He applied about three times; never got called.... So finally, we kind of traced the thing down, and I got another friend, a Black friend who had come out [to Raytheon] to work — for her husband to also apply. And they applied, [but] never heard from them [Raytheon]. And we knew other people who had applied — white — who had applied the same day and who had been taken.... So the two of us took the case to the then-head of ... the FEPC. And that was headed at that time by a man by the name of Elwood McKinney. And Elwood, who never lacked in zest, ... saw this as a good opportunity and a clear case of discrimination. And the next day, when I went in to work, it was almost as though the FBI was there. There were inspectors and people talking all over the place! And my husband was hired two days later."

Houston was soon elected shop steward in the local union at Raytheon, a position that helped prepare her for the many public service positions she was to hold in coming decades. She was at that time President of her neighborhood Home and School Association, one of various groups trying to cope with problems in the public schools.

Politics after Curley

Some saw John Hynes' defeat of Mayor James Michael Curley in '49 and Hynes' inauguration at the beginning of the new decade as a hopeful sign. Certainly that was true of Victor Bynoe, whom Hynes promptly named a Boston Street Commissioner. Bynoe says of Mayor Hynes:

"Hynes was the first guy that did the right thing.... He says, 'Victor,' he says, 'we have a job to do here.' He says, 'Your community has been really wrecked because the boys who grab everything have given nothing to the people. And we've got to rebuild the thing somehow.'"

In 1950 Hynes appointed Beulah S. Hester to be the first Black on the Board of Overseers of Public Welfare. At the end of the decade, he would appoint Victor Bynoe to the Board of the Boston Housing Authority.

One person who was not happy about having Hynes in City Hall was Shag Taylor, who had again supported Curley. Apparently, Taylor also lacked great influence in the '50s at the State House, where first Democrat Paul Dever and then Republican Christian Herter sat in the governor's seat through most of the decade.

When Dever decided to follow Gov. Robert Bradford's example and appoint a Black attorney to the judiciary [as already noted, Bradford had made Bruce Robinson the first Black Massachusetts Judge in this century], he did not turn to Shag Taylor for advice. Instead, he offered the position to Victor Bynoe. The ultimate beneficiary was Ned Gourdin, a Harvard-trained Black lawyer from the West Indies, Bynoe recalls:

"There was an opening in the Roxbury District Court. And Paul Dever and his henchmen wanted me to consider it. And I said 'No, that job goes to Gourdin; make him the judge in the Roxbury District Court.' ... Julian Rainey and all those old-time lawyers were looking for a job, but I said, 'No, forget about them, those guys have had their day. They've done nothing.... I'll step aside only for Ned Gourdin."

Bynoe also indicates that at the time — the late '40s, early '50s — Shag Taylor and Julian Rainey were no longer working together:

"I don't think he [Shag Taylor] was fighting for Julian, because by this time they were miles apart. They were close buddies years before."

Taylor was not, however, without influence in the '50s, as indicated by his election as an Alternate Delegate to the Democratic Convention in 1952.

Martin Luther King and Coretta Scott

The person Mayor Hynes appointed to the Welfare Board in 1950 — Beulah S. Hester — was a social worker and wife of Rev. William H. Hester, then Pastor of Twelfth Baptist Church, where a young Boston University theology student named Martin Luther King Jr. worshipped and occasionally preached.

Robert Coard, who would become Director of Action for Boston Community Development (ABCD), was also at Boston University in the early '50s, and his wife, Ida, was a classmate of Coretta Scott at New England Conservatory. Coard, who was born and grew up on the island of Grenada, recalls how he and his wife, whom he married soon after arriving in Boston, helped bring Coretta Scott and Martin Luther King together:

"Because there were very few Black students at the Conservatory in those days, my wife and Coretta became quite friendly. And we use to drive and pick her up on Chestnut Street [Beacon Hill], and we used to go to dinner and to shows and other things. And her boyfriend at the time ... used to conk his hair, and ... when the four of us went to a restaurant or any nice place, he acted like a clown. And so Ida and I talked to Coretta and said, 'Look, Coretta, you've got to do better than this.' And she said to us, 'Well... you've got to help....' And we said, 'Okay....'

"And then one other part-time student at the time, was ... Mary Powell.... We just had a discussion with her..., and between us we said that we needed to get these two together.... So Mary says, 'Well, I'll do the actual introduction, Bob.' ... And we settled on Martin Luther King at that meeting we had at my house."

Malcolm X

At about the time King and his future wife were getting acquainted in Boston in 1952, Malcolm Little was being paroled from a Massachusetts prison after serving six years of a 10-year sentence for burglary. Little, who had converted in prison to the teachings of Elijah Muhammad, would soon change his name to Malcolm X and eventually become famous as national spokesman for the Nation of Islam. Like Martin Luther King, Malcolm Little spent only a few years in Boston — but like King, he would put his stamp on a movement that would profoundly affect African-Americans in and out of Boston for decades to come.

By 1954, Malcolm X was founding Nation of Islam Temple 11 in Boston, Temple 12 in Philadelphia, and Temple 7 in New York City.[35]

By 1955, Martin Luther King was leading the Montgomery bus boycott — with Coretta Scott King at his side. During the second of two return visits to Boston in the mid-'60s, Martin Luther King toured Roxbury and showed support for school boycotts led by Black parents, students, and community activists. A news reporter asked King if he had any special memories of his years at Boston University, where he lived in a Divinity School dormitory:

"I remember very well trying to find a place to live," said King, who had just spoken to the state legislature about housing problems in the Commonwealth. "I went into place after place where there were signs that rooms were for rent. They were for rent, until they found out that I was a Negro, and suddenly they had just been rented."[36]

King was fortunate to live in a university dormitory — something, Robert Coard recalls, that was not possible for Coard's wife-to-be — and presumably not possible for Coretta Scott:

"Boston, by the way, was an extremely prejudiced place, including the schools at that time, because my wife was denied permission to live in the dormitory.... She could not get a room at the dormitory, which was on Hemenway Street...."

The YWCA

The fact that the '50s was a conservative period in American politics doesn't mean there were no significant breakthroughs in the decade.

For instance, with prodding from the national YWCA and from Lucy Mitchell, the Boston YWCA gradually integrated its facilities. Mitchell was on the board of the Boston YWCA during the late '40s and early '50s. The last program to desegregate during her tenure was the swimming pool.[37]

The opening of the YWCA pool must have been particularly satisfying to Melnea Cass, who had quit Boston's YWCA Board in the '40s over the issue of Blacks using the pool. Mrs. Cass would live to see the Clarendon Street YWCA named in her honor in 1976.[38]

Urban renewal: South End

By 1950, the City of Boston was near the bottom of an economic slump that left the city in an advanced state of decay. Since the late '20s, not a single office building had been constructed in downtown Boston.[39] Commercially the city appeared to be dying. The port was no longer competing with New York, the textile mills were moving south, and the well-to-do were moving to the suburbs. As a consequence, Boston became the primary guinea pig for faddish federal experiments in urban renewal.

Urban renewal in Boston began during the early '50s in the New York Streets area of the South End, where Mel King grew up. Here is how he describes his childhood neighborhood:

"Up and down Harrison Avenue there were shops and stores of all descriptions and families who lived over them in apartments upstairs. On the corner of Seneca and Harrison, there was an Armenian store with olives in barrels out front, and a fish market next door. The next block down on the corner of Oneida was Leo Guiffre's bakery, I think. There was a synagogue on Oswego. Bikofsky's bakery was on the corner of Lovering and Harrison, and Saroka's Drug Store a block down on Davis Street."[40]

In 1953, King's parents were notified that this "slum" was going to be "renewed." After demolishing the buildings in the area, the city let it stand empty several years, then "redeveloped" it as commercial property. The offices of the *Boston Herald* newspaper now occupy the ground the King family once called home. Mel King, who would lead the fight against unbridled South End development for decades to come and serve in the state legislature from 1973 to '82, watched in the '50s as his old neighborhood fell to the wreckers piece by piece:

"In the middle fifties, I was working at Lincoln House, coaching kids in the South End. I could trace the movement of families from one neighborhood to another by the route I had to go to pick up the kids I worked with. As one area was demolished, families were forced to move on. From the New York streets, families generally moved to Castle Square; from there, when it was renewed, most white families went to South Boston, Dorchester, and Jamaica Plain. Black and Portuguese families moved to Washington Park, Lower Roxbury, and North Dorchester. Some families have had to move four and more times in the face of renewal pressure."[41]

King's parents received some assistance from the government, but were stuck paying higher rent for another apartment in the South End. Some, of course, were less fortunate and had to seek public housing, which was hard to find and could be hazardous for Blacks, as Ed Cooper recalls:

"In 1952, the first Black woman who moved into Mission Hill, a senior citizen, the first night she was moved in there, she was stoned."

The NAACP

The Boston NAACP started off the decade by hosting the 41st Annual NAACP Convention June 20-25, 1950, at Union United Methodist Church on Tremont Street. Most of the 500 delegates — all the Blacks from out of town — had to be housed in private homes. No respectable Boston hotel would register Blacks. The NAACP delegates passed an anti-communism resolution by a vote of 309 to 57.

In 1949 and '50, the branch President was Florence Lesueur, the first woman in the country elected to head a branch of the NAACP. Muriel Snowden considered Lesueur's election significant for another reason:

"... When I came to Boston, Mrs. Lesueur was running for President and ... Julian Steele. And it was a very open thing that Julian represented the 'silkstocking' group in the Black community, and Flossie represented 'the people.' "[42]

In 1952, the NAACP awarded Rosa Brown, the mother-in-law of Melnea Cass, a "Life Membership" in honor of her 25 years of service to the local branch. For more than 20 years, Rosa Brown had led the chapter in finding new members.

In 1953, a publication of Boston's NAACP branch states:

"Through the efforts of the Housing Committee, tenant segregation in public housing was eliminated in 1951. But activities of our Branch did not stop there... In conjunction with other civic organizations, a brochure containing information on who is eligible for housing, how and where to apply, was prepared and distributed through churches, civic organizations, settlement houses and other places as a public service. We have also discussed employment in public housing for Negroes with many city officials. We strongly urge integration in personnel, of the city officials. We strongly urge integration in personnel, of the Boston Housing Authority."[43]

The above statement may appear naive and overly optimistic from the perspective of the 1980s, but it is proof at least that segregation in Boston's public housing was on the NAACP agenda.

In 1953, the branch was involved in the hiring of a Black waiter at the Meadows Restaurant in Framingham, marking "the first time in Massachusetts ... that a major restaurant catering to white clientele had employed white and colored waiters in the same dining room."[44]

Urban renewal: Roxbury

Amanda Houston grew up in the '30s and '40s in a lower Roxbury community that completely disappeared by the early '70s. Houston says the area was "BRA'd to death," starting back in the early '40s when city officials began to talk about pulling down the elevated Washington Street trolley tracks to "revitalize" the area:

"It was decided by someone that they were going to take the 'elevated' down and they were going to rehab this area from Northampton Street to Dudley Street, from Washington Street over to Columbus Avenue. And suddenly services began to pull out, schools began to be closed, businesses began, of course, to lose their customers and began to close and move out.... It was a gradual death ... over a 20-year period....

"The actual deterioration started in or around 1952, when the BRA [Boston Redevelopment Authority] really began to take over and to not rebuild — to just let things lay. They would take houses — people would sell houses to them, or abandoned houses — and they'd knock them down and just let the grass grow. It was the first time we began to see empty overgrown lots, dirty lots. And we began to see dirty streets and the lack of services.... I remember my mother going to meetings and her friends going to meetings with the BRA, saying, you know, 'When are you going to take action, when are you going to do this?' "

During the Washington Park Urban Renewal Project that would clear a wide swath through another section of Roxbury in the '50s and '60s, there was more effort to consult with residents than there had been during urban renewal in the South End. Nonetheless, the BRA's project was highly controversial. It included Haskins Street, where young Michael Haynes and politician Lawrence Banks had lived. Here is Haynes' recollection of the renewal project:

"The BRA's plan was to tear down everything and build anew, and later on they found out that this was grossly wrong. And some of the properties that were torn down were good properties, far better than a lot of the stuff that has gone — certainly far better than the stuff you see here in Warren Gardens [a large housing development of the '60s]."

Much of the area that was redeveloped was "a very, very close community," Haynes recalls:

"There was a lot of bitterness. I think I shared a little of it myself. I know my mother did; it nearly killed her."

Much of the redevelopment came in the 1960s. By this time, Robert Coard was a BRA employee, doing research on the effects of urban renewal in Roxbury:

"I studied and wrote reports to Ed Logue [Director of the BRA] on the damage that was being done, and he used to stamp "Super-confidential" and "so-many copies" [on the reports].... Well, I think both Ed Logue and the Mayor at the time, John Collins, who was a conservative and still is, were very much into achieving the urban renewal — come hell or high water. And they would ride over any local objections in order to achieve what they considered a better community, which was nice spanking new housing. And they did not have the kind of regard for the human disaster that occurred in terms of the removal of lower-income people who were in the communities."

Freedom House, under the Snowdens, signed a lucrative contract with the BRA to organize Roxbury neighborhoods targeted for renewal in the Washington Park project. Otto Snowden says he saw no other way to improve the area:

"We decided that you couldn't plant flower boxes and make the community better. You had to have some basic changes: new buildings, schools, streets — plow everything. That's why we supported urban renewal.

"But see, the reason why there was some criticism was because they had to take some homes. And those who lost their homes — although they got tremendous prices for them, they were never bailed out. But nobody wanted to give up their home. And then, too, even though they got this money, to buy something equivalent elsewhere, it would have cost that much more. So that was part of the problem."

Otto Snowden also bemoans the fact that the federal government never provided the money to finish the project. Muriel Snowden, who spoke of "documentation to show that 2,000 people participated in the planning of Washington Park,"[45] also remarked:

"When we found out that urban renewal was no longer viable, that there was no way to get Washington to put the money into this community that it needed in order to finish, there was no sense in hanging in there, you're just spinning your wheels. So you move out, knowing that there are unfinished pieces."[46]

Otto Snowden was, nonetheless, satisfied with what the community got from urban renewal:

"What did the Black community get? They got the MDC swimming pool. We got our parks done over. We got the Boys Club, new Boys Club. We got the YMCA. We got two housing-for-the-elderly projects, the new Court House. All that was part of the Washington Park renewal plan."

Royal Bolling Sr. agrees substantially with Snowden:

"Well a lot of people have complained and protested against what happened in the Boston Redevelopment Authority in its early years. But the condition of the city was in such a shape that something had to be done. Some direction had to be taken. And it's one of those things that it's easier to see the mistakes after the fact than it is before. I've always thought — and still think — that it was a positive influence for Roxbury."

When Amanda Houston finally saw the heavy steel elevated Orange Line tracks removed from Washington Street in 1988, she wrote the following in an article for Boston College Magazine:

"My mother knew in the early 1950s that the El was slated to come down. Along with other members of her community, she looked forward to the day when the shadow would be removed from Washington Street, believing that the neighborhood would benefit. But the El was not removed then; the neighborhood was not improved. In fact, the opposite happened. It was destroyed by uncertainty.... The comfortable working-class, low-income residential area located between Dudley and Northampton Streets along Washington Street did not survive to reap the benefits of this bright new Washington Street. It died 15 years before the structure finally came down."[47]

Afterword

It is tempting to end this anecdotal excursion through past decades with a note about the irrevocable nature of human progress, because Blacks in greater Boston made enormous strides toward freedom and equality over this 40-year span. If public schools deteriorated, college opportunities increased, occupations opened up, and Black politicians were winning some elections.

The broader historical view is less conclusive. In terms of elected officials serving in state and local government, for instance, Black Bostonians of the '50s had only succeeded in recapturing toeholds in the City Council and the state legislature that had been lost around the turn of the century.

I am reminded of something John O'Bryant said in one of the interviews that made this narrative possible. Referring to the fact that he was assigned to a racially mixed unit when drafted into the Army during the Korean conflict in 1952 — rather than the segregated Army of the two world wars — O'Bryant termed the change "a significant shift, but not a major one," because there were still plenty of racial problems:

"I wasn't all that enthusiastic about the service. But I did my job, and did it to the best of my ability. And although there were racist occurrences within the military, it was just part of the turf. I mean that you did it with the whole idea that the longest day has an end."

That seems to have been the nature of progress from the '20s through the '50s — it was slow and inconclusive. Blacks in Boston were striving for full citizenship, but could never feel completely satisfied with the progress they made, because so much more was clearly needed. Nonetheless, they fought to overcome the injustices they inherited, knowing that the steps they took — however modest — would make greater strides possible for their children and grandchildren.

Endnotes

1   King, Mel, *Chain of Change: Struggles for Black Community Development* (1981), Page 4

2   Mitchell, Lucy, interviewed in Black Women Oral History Project, Schlesinger Library, RadcliffeCollege, Page 74

3   Fox, Stephen R., *The Guardian of Boston: William Monroe Trotter* (1970), Pages 264-5

4   Ibid., Page 240

5   Hayden, Robert C., "Boston's NAACP History: 1910-1982" (1982), Pages 3-4

6   Fox, op. cit., Page 254

7   Worthy, Dr. William, "The Story of the Two First Colored Nurses to Train in the Boston City Hospital", a 15-page booklet printed in 1942, Page 9

8   Ibid., Page 14

9   Kountze, M. Doc, reprinted with permission of the historian from his book, *This Is Your Heritage*, copyright © (1978), Page 372

10   Worthy, op. cit., Pages 14-15

11   Cass, Melnea, interviewed in Black Women Oral History Project, Schlesinger Library, Radcliffe College, Pages 64-5

12   Trout, Charles H., *Boston: The Great Depression and the New Deal* (1977), Page 177

13   Ibid., Page 193

14   Thernstrom, Stephan, *The Other Bostonians: Poverty and Progress in the American Metropolis, 1880-1970* (1973), Page 179

15   Kountze, quoting the Boston Globe, op. cit., Pages 472-3

16   Trout, op. cit., Page 298-9

17   Franklin, John Hope, *From Slavery to Freedom* (third edition, 1967), Page 527

18   Ibid.

19   Trout, op. cit., Page 299

20   Trout, op. cit., Pages 191-2

21   Bennett, Lerone Jr., *Pioneers in Protest* (1968), Page 22

22   Trout, op. cit., Page 264

23   Hayden, op. cit., Pages 4-5

24   Buni, Andrew and Rogers, Alan, *Boston: City on a Hill* (1984), Page 132

25   Snowden, Muriel, interviewed in Black Women Oral History Project, Schlesinger Library, Radcliffe College, Page 5

26   Quoted from Brian Doyle's article, "The Passion of Dave Nelson" in Fall 1988 Boston College Magazine, Page 54

27   Ibid.

28   Hayden, Robert C., "Faith, Culture and Leadership, A History of the Black Church in Boston" (1982), Page 37

29   Thernstrom, op. cit., Page 179

30   For more information on the Banks campaigns, see James Jennings chapter, "Black Politics in Boston, 1900-1950" in *From Access to Power: Black Politics in Boston*, edited by Mel King and James Jennings (1986).

31   Jennings, James, quoted in the Boston Globe, Sept. 27, 1982

32   King, op. cit., Page 12

33   Jennings, Page 17, (see Endnote 30)

34   Thernstrom, op. cit., Page 179

35   Malcolm X, with assistance of Alex Haley, *The Autobiography of Malcolm X* (1964), Page 215

36   Quoted by David J. Garrow in *Bearing the Cross: Martin Luther King Jr. and the Southern Christian Leadership Conference* (1986), Pages 422-3

37   Mitchell, op. cit., Pages 48-9

38   Cass, op. cit.

39   Lupo, Alan, *Liberty's Chosen Home: The Politics of Violence in Boston* (1977), Page 86

40   King, op. cit., Page 20

41   King, op. cit., Page 22

42   Snowden, op. cit., Pages 61-2

43   Hayden, Robert C., "Boston's NAACP History: 1910-1982" (1982), Page 9

44   Ibid., Pages 8-9

45   Snowden, op. cit., Page 61

46   Snowden, op. cit., Page 64

47   Houston, Amanda, "Beneath the El," article in Summer 1988 Boston College Magazine, Pages 20-1

Index of Oral History Interviewees

A Curriculum Guide for High Schools and Colleges

prepared by
Robert C. Hayden
Educator, Historian, Author

For each of the four decades covered in *Witness: An Oral History of Black Politics in Boston, 1920-1960,* this guide provides:

— Background information.
— A chapter summary.
— Social studies concepts and topics.
— Questions for discussion.
— Activities.
— Suggested reading.

Like any history text, this book represents a number of choices from the vast repository of available materials, interpretations, and methods of historical study. A student reading the manuscript will gain:

❖ Basic facts concerning events and personalities in Boston's African-American history.

❖ The chronology of major events in this history.

❖ A sense of history as seen from a variety of viewpoints.

❖ A knowledge of how historical events in Boston affected and were influenced by Black people in Boston.

❖ An appreciation of Boston's ethnic and cultural diversity.

❖ A sense of the relationship between historical events and current events.

❖ Skills in locating, processing, and interpreting historical information.

Teaching Boston History

Bostonians are fortunate to live in a city that reflects many of the major themes in American history and offers students so many historical resources. Such themes as the American Revolution, immigration and migration, civil rights, urban development, ward politics, and a host of contemporary issues are readily accessible. The ethnic and cultural diversity of Boston helps students link U.S. history with their own community history. To omit local history would mean sacrificing an excellent opportunity to bring American history to life.

There is a growing awareness among educators, historians, and others that traditional history courses have too often reflected an almost exclusively white male perspective and concentrated on the activities of powerful elites to the exclusion of common people and non-whites. Many Boston teachers, parents, and administrators have expressed their concern that the curriculum avoid this path.

For this reason, Boston public schools' U.S. history objectives stress a multicultural approach. The objectives require students to integrate the traditional study of major political events with the history of Black, Hispanic, and Asian peoples, as well as Native Americans, women, and those Americans who have not kept literary records. Students are also asked to consider events from different vantage points, to examine different interpretations of the same events, and to engage in critical thinking about history.

This book and curriculum guide are designed to help implement the above philosophy and goals.

Chapter One —
Atmospherics and Childhood Memories

Background Information:
In 1900, Boston's Black population was 11,591 — 2.1 percent of the total city population. By 1910, it was 13,564 — 2.0 percent of the total. In 1920, Blacks numbered 16,350 — 2.2 percent of the city population. Boston was somewhat distinctive in attracting less than its share of Black newcomers during the Great Migration of Blacks from South to North during World War I and its aftermath.

Boston was also distinctive in that it was the first city in the country to have a branch of the National Association for the Advancement of Colored People (NAACP). By 1920, the branch had 2,700 members — Black and white.

Chapter Summary
❖ Illustrates the problems faced by Blacks in the military service in the early 1900s.
❖ Explores the racial climate for Blacks in and around Boston in the early 1900s.
❖ Sets the stage for exploring and understanding the politics of the Black community in Boston in the 1920s.

Social Studies Concepts and Topics: discrimination, prejudice, justice, injustice, segregation.

Questions for Discussion
1. What are some of the earliest memories you have of the city or place where you first lived in? Did you or members of your family face any type of discrimination? If so, how was it dealt with?
2. What did Henry Quarles and Elma Lewis face as young students in Boston during the 1920s?
3. How would you describe the racial atmosphere in Boston for Black men and women at the beginning of the 1920s?

Activities

1. Study issues of *The Guardian* newspaper between 1915 and 1920 at the Boston Public Library to learn about Black people and historical events just prior to 1920.

2. Interview a Black person who migrated to Boston between 1920 and 1940. Find out why he or she came to Boston. What did he/she experience?

3. View the slide-tape production "William Monroe Trotter (1872-1934): One-Man Protestor" available at Boston College and at the central library of the Boston Public Schools. There is a teaching-learning guide for the production.

Suggested reading:

The Guardian of Boston: William Monroe Trotter, Stephen R. Fox, Atheneum, New York, 1971.

Faith, Culture and Leadership: A History of the Black Church in Boston, Robert C. Hayden, published by Boston Branch NAACP, 1983.

Black Bostonia, Boston 200 Neighborhood History Series, 1976.

Chapter Two —
The 1920s: Forces in the Black Community

Background Information

Between 1920 and 1930, Boston's Black population went from 16,350 to 20,574. Informal politics "took hold" during this decade, led by Silas Taylor, who came to Boston in the early 1920s from Virginia. By 1925, he and his brother, Balcolm, owned and operated the Lincoln Drugstore on Tremont Street in lower Roxbury. This was not an ordinary store. The business served as headquarters for Black political aspirants, entertainers, and business and professional people. For the Taylor brothers, helping Blacks from the South find jobs, getting them to register to vote, and helping them find housing was a mission.

Chapter Summary

— Explores how Blacks in Boston in the 1920s responded to racial injustice and oppression.

— Describes generally the Garvey movement in Boston.

— Discusses the civil rights stances and actions of William Monroe Trotter, a fiery Black newspaper publisher and activist in Boston between 1901 and 1934.

— Explores the controversy over Plymouth Hospital in Boston, a hospital established for Black people in 1908.

— Describes the relationship between Boston's Mayor James Michael Curley and the Black community.

Social Studies Concepts and Topics: integration, separatism, civil rights, protest.

Questions for Discussion

1. What were the goals of Marcus Garvey?

2. Why was Silas (Shag) Taylor viewed positively and negatively by Black people in Boston?

3. Do you think William Monroe Trotter and Dr. William Worthy should have opposed the expansion of Plymouth Hospital in the 1920s? Why?

Activities

1. Study issues of *The Boston Chronicle* newspaper during the 1920s on microfilm at the Boston Public Library. What Black community issues and events did it discuss? Compare it to Trotter's paper, *The Guardian*, during this period.

2. On March 4 each year, the Equal Rights League, founded by Trotter, holds an outdoor memorial service in downtown Boston to commemorate Crispus Attucks, a Black man who was first to die in the Boston Massacre. Make a plan for you and your students to participate in this annual event.

3. Write a poem about William Monroe Trotter?

Suggested Reading:

1. *Marcus Garvey: Hero.* Tony Martin, Majority Press, 1983.

2. *Black Moses: The Story of Marcus Garvey and the*

Universal Negro Improvement Association. Edmund D. Cronon, University of Wisconsin Press, Madison, 1969.

3. *Trotter Institute Review*, Volume 2, No. 1, Winter 1988, a special issue dedicated to the life and work of William Monroe Trotter published by the William Monroe Trotter Institute, University of Massachusetts at Boston, edited by Dr. Wornie L. Reed.

4. *The Other Bostonians: Poverty and Progress in the American Metropolis, 1880-1970.* Stephan Thernstrom, Harvard University Press, Cambridge, 1973.

5. *I'd Do It Again: A Record of All My Uproarious Years.* James Michael Curley. Prentice Hall Inc., 1957.

Chapter Three —
The 1930s: Jobs, Jobs, Jobs!

Background Information

Between 1930 and 1940, Boston's still small Black population grew from 20,574 to 23,679 — accounting for only 3.1 percent of the total city population by 1940. The great majority were crowded in the South End-lower Roxbury neighborhoods.

Southern Black migrants who came to Boston in the early 1900s found themselves on the lowest rungs of the occupational ladder. In 1900, 12 out of 13 worked in blue-collar jobs — most as unskilled laborers, janitors, waiters, servants, and porters. Even the majority of northern and Boston-born Blacks were in the low-skilled, low-paying jobs during the early 1900s. In 1920, 54 percent of the Black males in Boston were in unskilled occupations; 20 years later, in 1940, 53 percent were still in the unskilled labor force.

Chapter Summary

❖ Explains the shift of many Black people from the Republican to the Democratic Party in the early 1930s.

❖ Gives examples of employment discrimination faced by Black people in Boston.

❖ Traces the development of political awareness in Boston's

Black community in the 1930s and '40s.
  ❖ Describes early public housing for Blacks in Boston.
  ❖ Outlines the work of the Boston NAACP in the '30s.

Social Studies Concepts and Topics: power, social change, political party politics.

Questions for Discussion

1. What types of discrimination did Black people in Boston confront in the 1930s? Give examples.

2. How did Wilfred Scott's approach to politics and jobs differ from that of Shag Taylor?

3. What strategies did Black people in Boston use to develop political power in the 1930s?

Activities

1. Visit the Schlesinger Library at Radcliffe College and study the oral history transcripts of Black women of Boston in the '20s, '30s, and '40s. For example: Melnea Cass, Lucy Mitchell, Muriel Snowden. Consult with Ruth Hill, Director of The Black Women Oral History Project at Radcliffe for use of the materials.

2. Invite retired Judge Harry Elam or former state Senator Royal Bolling Sr. to speak to your class, civic, or church group about Boston politics in the '30s and '40s.

3. View the film, "Moving in Boston," available at the Museum of Afro-American History, Joy Street, Boston. It gives an historical overview of neighborhood and occupation changes for Blacks in Boston.

Suggested Reading:

"Boston — Blacks and Progressive Politics," James Jennings, in *The New Black Vote,* edited by Rod Bush, Synthesis Publications, San Francisco, 1984.

"The Age of the Bosses," Chapter 6 in *Bibles, Brahmins and Bosses, A Short History of Boston,* Thomas H. O'Connor, Boston Public Library, 1976.

Boston's Workers, A Labor History, James R. Green, Trustees of the Public Library of the City of Boston, 1979.

Chapters Four and Five —
The '40s: Interlude for World War II and
On the Home Front

Background Information

In contrast to their hopes before World War I, Black Americans had no illusions about the benefits they might gain from World War II. Blacks had to fight for equal treatment overseas and at home. Although the Army was still segregated, the Selective Service Act of 1940 forbade discrimination in drafting and training, and Black officers trained in the same schools as whites.

By the end of World War II, few defense and defense-related industries were without at least some Black workers. There was a large migration of Blacks out of the South to the northern defense-industry communities. Boston's Black population began to surge in the early '40s, and by 1950 Boston had a population of 40,157, a 70 percent increase in just ten years.

Chapter Summary

❖ Black men recount the discrimination they faced in the military during World War II.

❖ Describes how Black leaders moved aggressively for jobs that had never been open to them.

❖ Illustrates growing dissatisfaction with de facto segregated schools and the deteriorating quality of schooling in the Black neighborhoods during the '40s.

❖ Describes the growing political sophistication of Boston's Black leadership in the '40s.

❖ Gives examples of housing discrimination.

Social Studies Concepts and Topics: boycott, urban renewal, bloc voting.

Questions for Discussion

1. What connection does Mel King make between city

---

charter reform in 1948 and urban renewal in the 1950s and '60s?

2. With the exception of Lawrence Banks (who served only three months of his elected two-year term on the Boston City Council in 1951), no Black person was elected to the Council or the Boston School Committee between the 1890s and the early 1970s. Why do you think this lack of elected political representation lasted so long?

3. In the past, the political process has been viewed as an avenue by which racial and ethnic groups could achieve upward mobility. Does this hold true for Black people in Boston today?

Activities

1. Interview an individual from each of the following groups about politics and community affairs in Boston after World War II: a Black citizen who migrated from a West Indian island, one who migrated from the South, and a "Black Bostonian." Use the same questions for each interviewee and compare their perceptions and responses.

2. Study issues of *The Guardian* and *The Boston Chronicle* on microfilm at the Boston Public Library for the 1945-1950 period. Compare the coverage of political issues and events of these two Black community newspapers by comparing headlines and editorials for the same dates.

Suggested Reading:
"Black Politics in Boston, 1900-1950," James Jennings, in *From Access to Power: Black Politics in Boston,* edited by James Jennings and Mel King, Schenkman Books Inc., Cambridge, Mass., 1986.
Boston's NAACP History, 1910-1982, Robert C. Hayden. Boston Branch NAACP, 1982.
The National Urban League, 1910-1940, Nancy J. Weiss. Oxford University Press, 1974.

Chapter Six—
The '50s: Gathering Steam

Background Information

Between 1896 and 1978, no Black person was elected to the Boston School Committee. A Dr. Samuel Courtney served on the Committee in 1896, and a Mr. Still served in 1875.

One of the "unsung heroines" who preceded the activist elected and non-elected politicians of the '40s and the '50s was Florence Lesueur. She was elected President of the Boston Branch NAACP in 1948 — the first woman ever elected to a branch presidency in the country. As early as 1941, she was petitioning the Massachusetts Bay Transportation Authority (MBTA) to hire Black bus drivers; she worked with the Boston Red Sox on the hiring of Black players and workers at Fenway Park. It was her energy and vision in leading the NAACP's Educational Counseling Committee in the late '40s and her work at the Harriet Tubman House that "built up the steam" for the '50s and '60s.

Chapter Summary

❖ Discusses the initial coming together of Black parents and the Boston NAACP for school improvement in Boston's Black neighborhoods.

❖ Tells about the final emergence of Black voices and representation in the General Court of Massachusetts.

❖ Describes the early political career of Edward W. Brooke, who was the first Massachusetts Black to serve as state Attorney General and United States Senator.

❖ Community activists describe having to defend themselves against charges that they were Communists.

❖ Discusses the experiences of Martin Luther King Jr. and Malcolm X in Boston.

❖ Long-time Boston residents reflect on the effect of urban renewal in South End and Roxbury neighborhoods.

Social Studies Concepts and Topics: "separate but equal"
doctrin, leadership, political empowerment,coalition politics, urban renewal.

Questions for Discussion

1. How did Black political activity and strategy change
between the 1920s and the 1950s?

2. What is a role model? Were there role models in Boston's
Black community during the four decades from 1920 to 1960?
Name some. Why do you consider them role models?

3. How did Black residents view urban renewal in the South
End-Roxbury neighborhoods?

Activities

1. Using census data and City of Boston records to find out
how many eligible Black voters there were in the 1940s, 1950s,
and 1960s. How many, or what percent, of the eligible voters
actually voted during these decades? Has the percentage
increased during the 1980s?

Suggested Reading:
Ed Brooke: Biography of a Senator, John H. Cutler, Bobbs-
Merrill, Indianapolis, 1972.
Chain of Change: Struggles for Black Community Development,
Mel King, South End Press, 1981.

Both Martin Luther King and Malcolm X lived in Boston in the
early '50s. Read biographies and autobiographies of both men
to learn how Boston affected them while they were residents.

Collecting Oral History

To create *Witness, an Oral History of Black Politics in Boston, 1920-1960,* the author makes extensive use of oral history. He interviewed many leaders and public officials, particularly those who were associated with major events.

We seldom have the privilege of looking back at a period of history with such an eye for its importance. It is even more unusual when most of the participants in that history are still alive to tell their stories. By personally exploring such history, you can learn how events affected the lives of your family and community before you were born. You may find some who were involved. Others perhaps may have been frightened or angered. By asking, you'll learn more about Boston history in an intimate and relevant way.

What is oral history?

Oral history involves collecting, through tape-recorded interviews, the spoken memories of a person's life. The oral history technique involves the gathering of personal perceptions and recollections of past events by persons with first-hand knowledge of those events.

Locating and selecting an interviewee

You should be able to find people living in Boston today who were involved in some way in the civil rights movement. Look for people who participated in marches, boycotts, freedom schools, or civil rights organizations. Talk with people in your church and consult with newspeople and those active in current civil rights groups. Visit your public library and review old newspapers to identify the civil rights issues, activities, organizations, and leaders in your area during the '40s, '50s, and '60s. See if you can locate people who participated in voter registration drives, the NAACP, urban renewal, electoral politics. When selecting your interviewee, don't assume that only the very old have a story to tell.

Arranging the interview

No matter who you want to interview, it is best to give them some time to prepare for the session. Even your immediate family and friends will provide more information if you let them know beforehand what the interview will be about, so they can give the subject some thought. You should also take the time to do some research yourself. Find out as much as you can about your interviewee and prepare your questions carefully.

Equipment and materials

You'll need a cassette tape recorder, three high-quality 60-minute cassettes, a hand-held microphone, a notepad and pen to jot down questions you may think of during the interview, and an extension cord or batteries for the recorder.

Preparing interview questions

An oral history interview is really a planned conversation between two people. You should have a well-thought-out and well-written questionnaire for your interview session. In order to ask intelligent questions and recognize important information given by the interviewee, you must do some background research on your topic from written accounts. Many of your questions should be based on your research.

Put your questions into a logical order. Be familiar with your questions and their order so you don't have to read them one by one during the interview. You don't want interviewees to feel that they are answering a questionnaire that could have been done in writing. Remember that a good interview is a conversation. You should be ready to ask questions that may not be on your prepared list. You want your interview to be open and spontaneous, so don't share the questions with your interviewee beforehand.

Guideline questions

Producers usually conduct a preliminary interview over the telephone to determine what special information the interviewees might be able to offer, whether they will be easy to interview, and whether they are good storytellers. You can save yourself a good deal of time by conducting such a pre-interview. Ask a few general questions that will help you focus your real interview. Here are some examples:

❖ What is your first memory of marching with Martin Luther King in Boston?

❖ Did you take part in any civil rights protests?

❖ Did you ever write a letter of support or concern to politicians or newspapers concerning civil rights?

If you are interviewing family members, you may want to know how they felt about these civil rights years, whether they participated or not. But if you want first-hand accounts of what people in your area were doing during this period, pre-interviewing will save you a great deal of time.

When you conduct the actual interview, your first goal should be to help the interviewee remember where he or she was during the period under discussion. Certain key moments in history have fixed themselves in the memories of the entire nation. Use these milestones to help take the interviewee back to the period you want him or her to talk about. For instance, you might ask:

❖ How old were you in 1954 when the Supreme Court outlawed segregated schools?

❖ Do you remember seeing Dr. King in Boston? Where?

❖ What were you doing when you heard the news that Shag Taylor had been killed?

❖ Do you remember the 1950 NAACP Convention in Boston?

Here are some additional guidelines to follow when conducting your interview:

1. Make sure that your interview takes place in an environment free of noise and distractions.

2. Set up your recorder efficiently and unobtrusively. Place the microphone on a soft surface, such as a magazine or book, to reduce background noise.

3. Explain the purpose of the session again to your interviewee before you start asking questions. To begin, record your stated purpose and the interviewee's name, the date, and the location of the interview. Check your recorder by playing back this information.

4. Ask brief, noncontroversial questions at the start.

5. Talk only when absolutely necessary; let the interviewee do the talking. You should hear yourself on the tape only when asking questions.

6. Do not ask questions that require a yes or no answer.

7. Do not interrupt the interviewee.

8. Keep the interview to approximately one hour.

9. Pause during the interview when you sense that the person you're interviewing needs to rest or think.

10. Follow your prepared questionnaire. Do not be concerned if the interviewee digresses from the questions; this often results in important information.

11. Adding good questions that are not on your questionnaire will require good listening.

12. Do not take notes while the interviewee is talking; take them at breaks before questions, or when the interviewee pauses.

13. Remember, the quality of your interview depends on your questioning to get the full story, the proper sequence of events, and specific details.

Transcribing oral history

An oral history tape is invaluable in itself for people to listen to years from now. Typed transcripts of tapes are even more valuable and easier to use for discussion and learning. The transcription should be verbatim — every word, pause, laughter, and false start should be included.

Once your interview is completed, you will want to transcribe the tape. Once you have done that, send a copy of your interview to the interviewee so that he or she can make any needed corrections or changes. This final version serves as your document.

The unpublished words of a person who grants an oral history interview are his or her own property. Permission to use the interview material, for whatever reason, should be obtained in writing at the start of the interview. Sample release forms can be found in the books listed below:

Books on oral history

Oral History: An Introduction for Students, by James Hoopes, University of North Carolina Press, 1979.
An Oral History Primer, by Gary L. Shumway and William G. Hartley, Primer Publications, P.O. Box 894, Salt Lake City, Utah, 1973.